MORAY HOUSE
AND CHANGE IN
HIGHER EDUCATION

To students, staff and
governors of Moray House,
past, present and future

MORAY HOUSE
AND CHANGE IN
HIGHER EDUCATION

Edited by
Professor Gordon Kirk

Principal, Moray House Institute of Education
Heriot-Watt University

1995

SCOTTISH ACADEMIC PRESS
EDINBURGH

Published by
Scottish Academic Press Ltd.,
56 Hanover Street
Edinburgh EH2 2DX.

SBN 0 7073 0741 4

British Library Cataloguing in Publication Data

A catalogue record for this book is available from
the British Library

Printed by Martin's the Printers Ltd., Berwick upon Tweed
and bound by Hunter & Foulis Ltd., Edinburgh

Contents

Preface

In 1985 *Moray House and Professional Education* was published. That was a collection of papers, written by members of staff at Moray House, to mark the college's 150th Anniversary and appeared during the celebration of that landmark in the history of the institution. That volume was not intended to be an in-house publication, which concentrated, introspectively, on internal politics and activities. Rather, the brief to which the authors wrote, invited colleagues to undertake a theoretical analysis of relevant professional issues and to consider how Moray House both responded to change and undertook initiatives that had an impact on professional practice.

After a further decade of significant institutional and professional change – perhaps the most significant of which is that Moray House is now the Institute of Education of Heriot-Watt University – it seemed appropriate to undertake a parallel exercise in institutional stocktaking. Accordingly, colleagues from each of the major areas of the Institute's work were invited to contribute to the present volume, working to the same brief as the authors in the 1985 volume. Again, the authors have all been heavily involved in the developments they describe and analyse, and the views they express are authentically their own. As in 1985, the papers will therefore reflect a diversity of views.

In the preface to the 1985 volume I expressed the hope that readers would encounter 'that capacity for self-criticism without which an institution committed to professional education has very little to celebrate'. Having served as Principal of Moray House since 1981, I can affirm that what in 1985 was a hope is now a confident expectation.

The creation of this book, like Moray House itself, is a tribute to team-work, and I gladly record my thanks to all of those whose willing co-operation brought it into being. The contributors must be thanked for making room for putting pen to paper in a hectic professional life. The typing of the various chapters was undertaken by colleagues on the secretarial staff of the Institute: Kate Dalgetty, Anne Linton, Sasha Noel, Lesley Spencer, Tabbi Scheffler, and Elspeth Wallace.

Mary Swinton not only typed and re-typed the drafts of my own contributions to the volume but, unerring and loyal as ever, incorporated adjustments that were required in response to my editorial work in other chapters. Dave Aikman was responsible for ensuring that the whole volume was prepared for transmission to the publishers. Alice Hamilton, my personal assistant, made sure that deadlines were met and that all the necessary details received the attention they required. Finally, I am extremely grateful to Douglas Grant of Scottish Academic Press for his positive support and generous advice in bringing the book into being.

To all of those mentioned, and to my colleagues on the staff whose achievements this book describes, I record my deep gratitude.

We are deeply indebted to the Bank of Scotland for its generous financial support in the production of this volume.

Professor Gordon Kirk
Principal.

December 1994.

1

The Changing Context of Higher Education in Scotland

Gordon Kirk

Introduction

On 17 July 1986, the Secretary of State for Scotland, Malcolm Rifkind, announced to Parliament that 'the training of physical education teachers, both men and women, will be centralised on the site of the present Dunfermline College of Physical Education and, accordingly, the training of men PE teachers at Jordanhill College of Education will cease. Dunfermline College will itself be merged with Moray House College of Education under a single governing body.' The enlarged Moray House was formally instituted on 1 April 1987. Then, in 1991, the Secretary of State agreed to the submissions from both institutions that Moray House should become the Institute of Education of Heriot-Watt University. These two landmarks reflected a wider restructuring of higher education in Scotland, one characterised by institutional re-definition, by mergers, and by other forms of academic association. In the decade following 1985, Scottish universities increased in number from 8 to 13; the total number of institutions was reduced from 25 to 21, and what in 1985 was described as 'an untidy and inadequately co-ordinated collection of institutions' (Kirk, 1985), standing in no obvious relationship to each other, became an integrated system operating within a common financial and constitutional framework under the aegis of the Scottish Higher Education Funding Council. The combined effect of these changes, some of them the outcome of ministerial decisions and some the product of bilateral negotiation, was a transformation of Scottish higher education. This chapter analyses the principal features of that transformation and Moray House's role within it.

The Scottish Tertiary Education Advisory
Council Report (1985)

The Scottish Tertiary Education Advisory Council (STEAC) was established in 1984, 'to consider and report on the future strategy for higher education in Scotland, including the arrangements for providing institutions with financial support and the general principles which should govern relationships between universities and other institutions'. That represented the government's second attempt in five years to systematise higher education in Scotland. In 1979, the Council for Tertiary Education in Scotland (CTES) had been established, with terms of reference relating directly to 'non-university tertiary education and its relationship with university education in Scotland'. In its report of 1981, CTES proposed a national authority for controlling non-university higher education, but made no more than token recommendations on the relationship between the new national authority and the universities (SED 1981). The Secretary of State rejected the CTES recommendation and for three further years the inadequacies of the system were reinforced: universities continued to register their concern at the University Grants Committee's (UGC) treatment of Scottish universities; in the central institution sector there was a strong feeling that these institutions were funded much less favourably than the universities and the divisions between the largest technological institutions, some of which sought polytechnic status, and the remainder, which were smaller and mainly monotechnic institutions, continued to exert themselves; and the colleges of education, reduced in number from 10 to seven in 1981, went on experiencing a decline in student numbers and staff with inevitable consequences for their morale. The difficulties experienced by these three sectors were reinforced by variations in funding, in governance, in their arrangements for course review and validation, and in many other ways.

The case for rationalisation and systematisation of higher education derived from an acknowledgement that student numbers were expected to decline as a result of a significant reduction in the size of the relevant age group, even when allowance was made for the increased participation of those who had formerly been under represented in higher education. In the light of that reduction, it was all the more important that resources were used wisely and well, and that a properly co-ordinated system was established. STEAC provided a further opportunity to take a strategic look at higher education as a whole.

Having acknowledged the importance of providing for increased opportunities in higher education, and for maintaining Scotland's educational self-sufficiency, STEAC turned to an analysis of the three principal sectors and their part in an integrated system. For the most part, STEAC's analysis was conservative. It concluded that, 'We do not consider that fundamental change is needed.' And again, 'We have broadly endorsed the present roles of the universities, the central institutions, the colleges of education, and the local authority sector of higher education in Scotland, and we propose that they should continue on similar lines.'

In line with that conservative assessment, STEAC affirmed the role of the universities as 'the sole providers of liberal arts education' and also 'the sole providers of degree courses in such areas as law, divinity, medicine, veterinary science and dentistry'. For their part, the central institutions were complimented on their 'responsiveness to employers' requirements', their 'strong vocational orientation', and their cost-effectiveness. While being anxious to avoid 'the immediate establishment by all CIs of sophisticated and expensive programmes of applied research', the Council recommended that CIs' engagement in research should be strengthened and supported through recurrent grant. Finally, it was recommended that the standing of the CIs could be enhanced through the establishment of a Scottish Institute of Technology, a mechanism for establishing greater collaboration between the institutions concerned. It was recommended that a feasibility study should be undertaken of this venture. It would include the five major CIs, plus the Scottish College of Textiles, and would involve co-ordination in planning, degree-granting status, and other functions.

It must be acknowledged that STEAC's analysis of the functional distinction between universities and central institutions was superficial. It focused mainly on differences in the level of research, in costs, and the alleged superiority of CIs as centres of vocational training. It was an analysis that, if anything, reinforced historical differences and therefore failed to acknowledge that, since both universities and central institutions operated at degree and postgraduate levels, there were grounds for questioning the 'binary' division between the universities on the one hand and non-university institutions on the other.

The same conservatism of philosophy is found in STEAC's treatment of the colleges of education. STEAC acknowledged that the integration of colleges of education within a university environment had attractions, not the least of which were 'the additional advantages which a more broadly based academic environment would bring'. But STEAC adduced several counter-arguments. Integration within the university sector might entail 'increased emphasis on the more academic and theory aspects of teacher training, and a reduction in the practical component'; it would involve increased costs through absorbing college staff into the higher salary structure of the universities, and the fact that teaching would continue on separate sites would mean that 'there would be little or no real integration'. Besides, the Council maintained that there were positive arguments for the *status quo*. The committee recognised the distinctive role of the colleges in Scotland and paid tribute to their in-service work for the teaching profession and their 'very significant contribution to curriculum development in the schools'. STEAC considered that 'the view of the teaching profession is certainly that the college of education system, as presently organised, has served Scotland well in the past and will continue to do so'. The committee noted the high regard in which the colleges were held by the teaching profession and commended the strong collaboration that had developed between the colleges, the teachers, and education authorities. Besides, the specialised nature of the colleges helped to engender a single-minded commitment, strengthening their sense of purpose and providing a sense of motivation for staff and students alike. Since 'no significant body of opinion' had recommended integration with other sectors, and since there was 'no evidence of dissatisfaction with the product of the present system', there was no case for major organisational change, although the colleges should be given support for research through recurrent grant.

While endorsing the institutional identity and separateness of the college of education sector, STEAC recognised that there was 'a structural problem currently facing the sector'. The evidence before it, mainly deriving from the report of the Controller and Auditor General in 1985, was that there was a considerable surplus of accommodation in the system. Despite the reduction from ten to seven colleges in 1981, the continued decline in the school population had necessitated a corresponding decline in the number of staff and students in the colleges. Convinced that the answer lay not in diversification of their activities, and that the quality of teacher education 'was to be protected by its concentration in thriving and specialist establishments', the Council concluded that some further contraction in the system was needed and that 'there seems to be no reason why the student population should not be accommodated in one denominational and three non-denominational colleges'.

Having examined the role and function of the three separate sectors, STEAC then turned to the key feature of its terms of reference, the relationship between institutions and sectors. The Council considered, but rejected, a number of proposals that would have brought the various sectors, or parts of them, into closer association through the creation of major federations of institutions formed on a geographical or functional basis. For the Council, what was required more than anything was national machinery which could facilitate strategic planning and development of higher education as a whole. While the minutes of the Council indicate that a majority favoured the establishment of a single over-arching body responsible for the planning and funding of higher education in Scotland, the university members could only agree if certain safeguards were established to ensure that universities continued to have access to funding from the Research Councils, to ensure that they continued to operate within a UK peer review system, and provided that the Scottish universities continued to attract, under SED control, the same proportion of the total funds for universities as they had enjoyed under the UGC. There was consensus on the committee for an over-arching planning body, and it was felt that that should be established 'at the earliest opportunity'. However, a national planning and funding body for all of higher education in Scotland should only be introduced when the three key conditions stipulated by the universities had been met.

The Response to STEAC

At one level the STEAC report was well received. The Glasgow Herald welcomed the measure of autonomy that was recommended for higher education in Scotland, seeing it as creating 'opportunities for genuine rationalisation as opposed to the crude retrenchment of recent years' (10 December 1985). On the same day, the Scotsman found the recommendations in favour of an over-arching council to be 'eminently reasonable and cogent'. However, it was left to the Times Higher Education Supplement to register an almost euphoric acclaim. Beneath the headline of 'Good News from Scotland', it went on, 'The report of the Scottish Tertiary Education Advisory Council, *Future strategy for higher education in Scotland*, which was published on Monday, attempts to impose a new order on this turmoil of changing circumstances. It is an impressive report which not only writes certainly an important chapter in the history of Scottish higher education, but also probably an influential footnote in that of British higher education. It makes radical recommendations, far more radical than many observers had predicted, but remains rooted in the reality of Scotland's present system.' It summarised the report as 'an impressive state paper'.

Towards the end of the consultation period at the end of March 1986 it became clear that, while Scottish opinion as a whole welcomed the recommendation for a national planning and funding body for higher education, the universities on the whole argued against that proposal. With the exception of Stirling and Strathclyde Universities, they opposed the Council's central recommendation and preferred to see funding continued through the University Grants Committee, fearing that the three guarantees mentioned in the report simply could not be met, and believing that the transfer of responsibility from UGC to a Scottish authority would 'erode their quality and international standing'.

At the same time, the universities recognised the need for a greater degree of national co-ordination of higher education provision, and the majority of them thought that could be achieved through the establishment of a sub-committee of the University Grants Committee or some other mechanism, such as a joint planning body for both university and non-university sectors. It was argued that such an arrangement was fully compatible with separate funding for the universities through the UGC on the one hand, and for the non-university sector through the SED on the other. Such an arrangement might operate for a number of years and, in the light of experience, the more radical step of creating a national planning and funding body could then be considered if it was thought necessary.

Unquestionably, the response to STEAC in Scotland was dominated by the recommendation that initial teacher education should be concentrated in four colleges. The opposition of the colleges themselves to this recommendation was predictable. They were joined in their opposition by a host of other bodies – The General Teaching Council, all four teachers' unions, academic staff unions, the STUC, the National Union of Public Employees, the National Union of Students, the Church of Scotland, and even the Salvation Army. In defence of the colleges, it was maintained that it was self-contradictory for STEAC to endorse, if not praise, the work of the colleges on the one hand, and then recommend their reduction on the other. Besides, the need for accessibility to in-service opportunities pointed to the need for the geographical dispersion of institutions. Most of the responses claimed that there appeared to be no educational reason for reducing the number of colleges. In a sustained and persuasively argued response, the Association of Lecturers in Colleges of Education in Scotland (ALCES) took issue with the three 'non-educational' arguments for closure. Firstly, it was argued that, if the closure of three colleges was intended to result in savings, the evidence on the savings had not been produced. Secondly, the arithmetical precision of the STEAC recommendation implied that data were available on the capacity of the various institutions. That, argued ALCES, was not the impression given by Mr James Scott, Secretary of the SED, during his cross-examination by the Public Accounts Committee in June of 1985 when, to his embarrassment, he was unable to give plausible answers to straightforward questions on the capacity of the colleges. Indeed, he was forced to acknowledge that the overall capacity of the college was simply not known, because no-one had devised an appropriate way in which that could be measured. Finally, ALCES argued, STEAC appeared to base its recommendation on the assumption of a peak student population 'of something over 5,000'. That did not square with the figure of 8,000 given by the Scottish Office to the Public Accounts Committee; nor did it take account of the increased number of students on in-service courses. All in all, ALCES argued that the recommendation on the college of education system rested on a somewhat 'wobbly tripod'.

A few bodies appeared to support the recommendation, most notably the college principals. It was their view that 'a measure of rationalisation of the college of education system is necessary and that it would be possible on a numerical basis to accommodate the population of pre-service students, as presently projected, in a smaller number of colleges'. Admittedly, the principals sought to qualify their view 'for reasons of prudence', pointing to the 'far-reaching educational effects of closure' and urging that these be weighed in comparison with other possible ways in which the existing space might be used.

However, the principals' was a somewhat lonely voice: the overwhelming weight of opinion was that the recommendation should be rejected.

The Ministerial Decision

Like the period of consultation which preceded it, the ministerial announcement on 17 July 1986 gave priority to the college of education question, a decision on an over-arching body being deferred 'until the government can form a clear view of the future funding arrangements for the Scottish universities'. The minister appeared to accept the principle that teacher education should continue to be placed in specialist institutions 'while not ruling out entirely the possibility of some other arrangement if circumstances appeared to warrant it'. He then intimated his decision on the recommendation to reduce the size of the college sector: Dundee and Aberdeen Colleges would merge; physical education at Jordanhill would transfer to the Cramond Campus of Dunfermline College, which would itself merge with Moray House under a single governing body. Finally, all colleges would be expected to make strenuous efforts to dispose of surplus capacity, and the Secretary of State would review the position in a year in the light of the progress made. If over-capacity remained a problem, 'site closures will then become inevitable'.

The debate which followed the announcement indicated clearly that, in going for the no-closure option and maintaining the existing geographical spread of teacher education sites, Mr Rifkind had produced an acceptable package. Predictably, the most critical comments were reserved for the proposed transfer of PE to Dunfermline College, and the virtual closure of the Scottish School of Physical Education. Mr Rifkind's justification for the move was that European legislation had made it necessary to end the separate training of male and female physical education teachers. Since there was no justification for two mixed physical education centres, one of the existing centres had to close. Dunfermline College was preferred because it was the only purpose-built physical education establishment in Scotland. As Mr Rifkind intimated to the House of Commons, the transfer was not intended 'to reflect in any way on the quality of the work done (at Jordanhill)': 'the educational arguments pointed overwhelmingly' to Dunfermline being the site for physical education.

The Moray House/Dunfermline College linkage had not been the policy objective of either institution: it was the result of a ministerial decision taken without consultation with the institutions. With hindsight, it can be seen to have been an astute way of minimising political embarrassment: the government clearly was under pressure to establish a single centre for physical education, there being no justification for two such centres. The decision to transfer physical education from Jordanhill to Dunfermline College was bound to create animosity at Jordanhill. However, the proposal to bring Dunfermline College within Moray House and to place it within a wider framework of teacher education was likely to temper the sense of victory. Finally, the decisions on the teacher education system enabled the Minister to achieve two objectives: the first was to reduce the overall number of colleges while, at the same time, recognising the importance of maintaining geographical spread of teacher education institutions for in-service purposes.

The Merger

The period following the Secretary of State's decision was marked by some hostile exchanges, some of them conducted in the press, between members of staff at Dunfermline College of Physical Education and the Director of SSPE. Most of these exchanges were expressions of opposition to the merger and the serious implications it had for physical education. Jordanhill College continued to campaign against the Secretary of State's decision. Even when formal discussions were initiated, in late August 1986, to give effect to the Secretary of State's decision, Jordanhill representatives attended on a 'without prejudice' basis, pending the outcome of their further discussions with the Secretary of State.

After preliminary discussion on 27 August, the first meeting of the Quadripartite Working Party took place on 4 September 1986. As its title suggests, the working party brought together representatives from the Scottish Education Department, Moray House, Jordanhill and Dunfermline College of Physical Education. The first meeting was not auspicious for it emerged that Moray House and Dunfermline College of Physical Education had differing interpretations about the kind of merger envisaged by the Secretary of State. For Dunfermline College, the aim was to create two relatively autonomous institutions operating under the aegis of an over-arching Board of Governors. For Moray House, the merger implied a more integrated institutional structure in which there would be a single principal, a single academic board, and a single governing body. It was agreed that ministerial clarification would be sought and, when it was disclosed that the Minister favoured the Moray House pattern, the formal business of the working party was able to proceed.

There followed a hectic series of meetings. Three sub-groups were formed to deal with course provision, accommodation and staffing, and each meeting of the working party received reports from the sub-groups and devoted time to the consideration of the title of the merged institution, the composition of the new Board of Governors, the senior academic staff structure, and other matters. As an indication of the pace of development, the interim report was published on 14 November, views were sought by 5 December, and the final report was published by 21 December 1986.

Inevitably, as the final report demonstrated, many issues were left unresolved, and it was left to what became known as the Merger Action Committee (MAC), a group of senior staff drawn from both institutions, to take forward many of the detailed matters to ensure that all the necessary arrangements were in place for the merger date of 1 April 1987. The Board of Governors of the new Moray House met on 3 April 1987 and a new chapter in the history of the institution was opened.

The University Connection

1987 marked the beginning of a new era, not simply for Moray House but for the whole of education in Scotland. In that year, a conservative government was returned after a third successive election victory and interpreted that victory as providing a mandate for the policies of the 'new right' in practically every sphere of public life. The new Minister for Education, Michael Forsyth, was an enthusiastic apostle of conservative philosophy and, with evangelical fervour, initiated a range of measures with the intention of restructuring education on market principles. Early in his period of office he declared, 'I believe in less government, in more local decision-making, and more local accountability.'

In line with that philosophy, a series of changes were introduced to non-university higher education in Scotland, which had the effect of removing bureaucratic constraints and strengthening the autonomy of individual institutions. The statutory machinery for national pay bargaining was dismantled; staffing arrangements were changed to allow institutions to make appointments without SED approval; the principal became the chief executive and, along with the Secretary of the Scottish Office, directly responsible to parliament; financial controls were loosened, giving institutions greater freedom while, at the same time, the overall framework of accountability was significantly reinforced. Institutions became recipients of grant-in-aid, implying that they could not expect to receive funds to cover all of their activities: they would require to assume responsibility for generating income for themselves and any surpluses made in a financial year could be retained.

Of course, some controls were continued, apart from those relating to accounting procedures: the Secretary of State retained the right to determine the number of students admitted to teacher education programmes, and also the right to approve teacher education courses. Nevertheless, the new climate was one in which institutions were encouraged to be self-reliant, innovative, and independent. It was a model of higher education rather different from the advice proffered to STEAC by several higher education institutions, including Moray House, that higher education in Scotland should be organised on the basis of a number of major federations of institutions based in the main cities. The government had rejected that scenario in favour of one in which diverse institutions openly competed in the market-place for students and for funds. The Secretary of State himself reinforced this in his address to principals in May 1990: 'I firmly believe that competition – or, to put it another way, choice for the consumer – is an essential and desirable element of a healthy service industry such as your own.' The message was put to the same audience with even more remarkable frankness by Michael Forsyth:

> The consistent thread running through all our policies for the grant-aided colleges is to emphasise that your future is in your hands. I believe that we are creating a climate which is bracing, healthy, and even stimulating. The fittest colleges will be able to go from strength to strength, and the remedy for the others will be in their own hands.

Government policy, then, in the year following 1987, was calculated to create a diverse system of higher education for Scotland, one that presented choice for consumers and nurtured inter-institutional competition. Institutions were empowered to determine their own lines of development. The 'arms-length' relationship between SED and institutions was acknowledged to offer institutions significant discretion. It therefore allowed the possibility that some institutions might 'seek to strengthen their position in the market-place by combining with institutions who were similarly inclined'. In the context in which institutions were free to work out their own salvation, it had to be acknowledged that some institutions might prefer to collaborate.

A second factor which influenced the decision to collaborate with Heriot-Watt University involved the threatened demise of the Council for National Academic Awards (CNAA). In 1981, when it embarked on a massive programme of course development and review, Moray House decided to look to CNAA as its validating body and there is no doubt that the institution benefited significantly from the rigorous approach to external validation and institutional review developed by the CNAA, and from participation in the national network of peer group evaluation sustained by CNAA. Throughout the '80s the CNAA's relationship with institutions changed. Following the Lindop Report (1985), certain institutions were 'accredited' and judged to be of sufficient maturity to take full responsibility for the validation and review of courses leading to CNAA awards, subject to institutional review by CNAA every seven years, and certain other safeguards, notably in connection with external examiners. There is no doubt that the polytechnics in England and Wales greatly valued the increased responsibility that was signalled by accreditation, and the demand for still further responsibility could not be indefinitely deferred. The government's White Paper, *Higher Education: Meeting the Challenge,* published in 1987, recognised the national role of these institutions and, believing that 'it is no longer appropriate for polytechnics and other colleges predominantly offering higher education to be controlled by individual local authorities', proposed that they be fully incorporated bodies with their own boards of governors. These provisions were enacted in the Education Reform Act of 1988, and the polytechnics and colleges became incorporated bodies from 1 April 1989.

Notwithstanding this development, the polytechnics aspired for still further institutional autonomy and the right to award their own degrees. If these institutions were successful in that regard, they would be responsible for 85% of the students enrolled on CNAA-approved courses. In that event, there would be an uncertain role for CNAA, and institutions that looked to CNAA for validation would be placed in some difficulty.

Therefore, while it was disclosed early in 1989 that there was to be a review of the work of the CNAA, it was clear that the issue for consultation involved the granting of degree-awarding powers to the polytechnics. That development made it essential for Moray House to seek to establish an alternative validating body to CNAA, especially when it began to be assumed that, under the new dispensation, institutions that did not have degree-granting powers would need to look to public sector institutions that did have that authority to have their courses validated.

At that time, an alternative validating body was available. The Scottish Council for the Validation of Courses for Teachers (SCOVACT) had been established by a consortium of Scottish universities and colleges of education in 1983 and, over the years, had provided an alternative to CNAA validation. While Moray House had been party to the establishment of SCOVACT it continued to seek validation through CNAA. SCOVACT was concerned only with the validation of courses for teachers and it was therefore not attractive to an institution that also sought a validating service for courses in social work, community education, and other areas. Besides, Moray House valued the rigorous approach to both external validation and institutional review developed by the CNAA, and feared that there might be a diminution in the externality and independence of that scrutiny if these activities were not undertaken on a UK basis but were undertaken by panels consisting mainly, or exclusively, of staff from Scottish institutions. These same considerations made SCOVACT an unattractive validating body for Moray House, even when the future of CNAA appeared uncertain. The Moray House response to that uncertainty was to turn to Heriot-Watt University for the validation of its programmes.

Other developments in Scotland helped to intensify the hostility of the higher education environment. In the course of 1987 and 1988, the Scottish Office showed a strong commitment to the creation of a formal mechanism for bringing non-university institutions into collaboration. That eventually became known as the Conference of Centrally-funded Colleges in Scotland, and SED officials attended all meetings of the new body after its formation in 1988. While the Conference may have been a valuable way of communicating with 17 different institutions and was ideal for the discussion of common problems, the SED's enthusiasm for the Conference could be open to other interpretations. For example, the Conference could be seen as the beginning of a total centralisation of the management of the non-university sector. Subsequent disclaimers have suggested that that interpretation of events was invalid. In May of 1989, Mr Forsyth reinforced this denial when he informed the

Conference that 'there is no blueprint being put together within SED offering a brave new world for higher education in Scotland'.

If there was no blueprint in the SED, one was being developed elsewhere. In October 1988, the Principal of Napier Polytechnic, Dr Bill Turmeau, who was then a member of the Moray House Board of Governors, wrote to the Secretary of State for Scotland arguing that Scotland had 'too many small, inefficient establishments with different sources of funding, different methods of management and control, and no vision for the future'. He advocated the reduction of Scotland's 25 higher education institutions to 10, over a period of five years. One of the 10 would be a merger of Napier and four other colleges in the Edinburgh area – Moray House, Queen Margaret College, Edinburgh College of Art, and the Scottish College of Textiles. That plan was not well received. One principal dismissed it as 'tendentious rubbish' and another as 'structurally incoherent'. However, these rebuttals did little to prevent an outbreak of 'merger mania'. At Moray House it was felt that, if, despite government disclaimers, there had to be institutional amalgamations, it would be preferable to associate with a university rather than a non-university institution.

All of these factors – the new climate of institutional self-determination, the threatened demise of the CNAA, the creation of the Conference, and the threats, unofficial or otherwise, of institutional amalgamation – helped to create a climate of uncertainty. The decision to seek an association with Heriot-Watt University was at least partly a response to that uncertainty.

At the same time, there were positive attractions in associating with a university, not the least of which was the academic endorsement of the work of the college. By 1989, Moray House had developed a range of undergraduate and postgraduate, including master's degree, programmes; the overwhelming majority of its students were on degree courses; a tradition of research was being established; and staff were heavily engaged in consultancy and other forms of scholarly activity. Moray House, indeed, had become the kind of institution that, in other countries, would have been fully incorporated within the university system. Staff of the institution had worked extremely hard over the years to build up the institution's academic and professional standing. A formal link with the university would be a public way of recognising these achievements, which were the direct product of the commitment and expertise of the staff.

Conscious that, if a formal link with Heriot-Watt University was established, Moray House would be breaking the mould of higher education in Scotland, informal approaches were made and the first meeting of representatives of the two institutions took place on 2 May 1989. That meeting was relatively brief and served to demonstrate a commitment on both sides to further discussion. At subsequent meetings, the wording of a 'Statement of Intent' was agreed for submission to the Board of Governors of the college, the Court of the university, and other bodies such as SED and the Universities Funding Council. The 'Statement of Intent', which was published on 28 June 1989, declared on behalf of both institutions 'that of their own accord they have initiated discussions to explore ways of fostering together closer academic collaboration and the prospect of a formal institutional linkage'. It proposed the establishment of a Joint Working Party to consider the most appropriate form of institutional association and to report by 31 March 1990. The report of the Joint Working Party, *Proposals for Linkage,* was received by both institutions on 9 March 1990. After outlining the academic and other advantages of a formal linkage for both institutions, the report identified two models of association: under Model 1 Moray House would retain its independence as a separately funded body with its own board of governors, its own academic board and principal, but students would become matriculated with the university and, on successful completion of their programme, would receive awards of the university. Model 2 implied a much closer form of association: under it there would be a single senate and a single court, which would be the legal employer of all staff; the college's board of governors would be abolished, as would its status as a separately funded institution. The Joint Working Party also considered the relocation of Moray House from its three existing sites to the Riccarton Campus.

The Joint Working Party recommended that, with the overall objective of establishing Moray House as a college of the university relocated at the Riccarton Campus, the Model 1 form of association should be adopted from September 1991 and a detailed financial appraisal should be undertaken in relation to the relocation of the college.

Since the report broke new ground in higher education, it was proposed that a formal consultative exercise should be undertaken inside both institutions and throughout the wider educational community, and, in the light of that consultation, a formal decision would be taken by both institutions in June of 1990. That consultation demonstrated overwhelming support for the Model 1 pattern of association, but serious reservations were expressed about the relocation of the institution, many believing that the city centre location of the Holyrood Campus should be maintained. The Moray House Academic Board was particularly concerned that a speedy decision was taken on Model 1 for, by that time, CNAA, sensing that its traditional validating role would disappear, had already initiated discussions with BTEC. That would have made CNAA validation less attractive since the merged validating body would not be responsible, as CNAA was, for university level awards only.

With the institutional positions clarified, it was then necessary to obtain the approval of the Secretary of State for Scotland. In subsequent discussion with the Department, two issues predominated: the role of the Secretary of State and the nature of the arrangements for external validation of courses. Both issues had been discussed in the 'Statement of Intent' and in the Joint Working Party report. In both, it had been made clear that the Secretary of State's approval was required and that 'the statutory rights of the Secretary of State for Scotland will remain unaffected by the institutional linkage'. Knowing the Secretary of State's commitment to external validation for teacher education courses, the Joint Working Party devoted considerable time to elaborating how externality of course scrutiny would be retained in the new arrangements. An Academic Advisory Committee would be established, drawing on experts from across the United Kingdom, and all validation decisions would be taken by a committee in which there was a majority of external representatives. The SED continued to seek reassurance on this matter, not realising that it involved a more stringent set of arrangements than those currently operated by the CNAA, which had gradually moved over the years to a form of joint validation in which the external influence had been reduced.

In due course, in January of 1991, the Secretary of State wrote to confirm that he had agreed to the Model 1 form of institutional linkage between Moray House and Heriot-Watt University and noted that both institutions had indefinitely suspended any discussion of the relocation of Moray House. The new arrangements had effect from the start of session 1991/92 and the first Moray House graduates to obtain Heriot-Watt awards did so in the graduation ceremonies in June/July 1992. In the course of that session, the various forms of academic collaboration were developed in line with the recommendations of the Joint Working Party report.

It is noteworthy that the establishment of Moray House as the Institute of Education of Heriot-Watt University was formalised only months before the government's White Paper of May 1991, *Higher Education: A New Framework*, which proposed the most radical changes in higher education this century. In a single remarkable document the government proposed the ending of the binary line; the winding up of the CNAA, following the recommendation of the review of that body in June 1990 that polytechnics should be given degree-awarding powers; the creation of separate funding councils for England, Wales, Scotland and Northern

Ireland; the introduction of quality audit and quality assessment machinery for all higher education institutions; and the extension of the title of 'university' to institutions that met certain defined criteria. In many ways, these changes were predictable and perhaps even inevitable. The binary distinction had, over the years, become less and less defensible as so-called 'public sector' institutions came to rival at least some universities in the range and quality of their work and, having achieved accredited status, were regarded by CNAA as if they were mature enough to be degree-awarding institutions. The release of polytechnics from local authority control and funding removed the single remaining justification for the binary policy. Despite that, dual funding arrangements continued through the Universities Funding Council on the one hand, and the Polytechnics and Colleges Funding Council on the other. But, even then, it was difficult to see the justification for maintaining two separate bureaucracies to perform identical functions for two sets of institutions.

With polytechnics clamouring for university status, and with the prospect of a merger of the two funding councils, the Scottish universities, which had felt none too secure with the UFC, were bound to consider their repatriation even if, at the time of the STEAC report six years earlier, that prospect had appeared not too attractive. The repatriation of the Scottish universities would inevitably bring them into relationship with Scotland's other higher education institutions, the 17 centrally-funded colleges. Within that latter group were those who persisted in seeking to defend the integrity and distinctiveness of the sector. But there were too many conflicts of interest for it to become a cohesive force. Furthermore, the mechanism devised by the Secretary of State for Scotland to advise him on higher education strategy in Scotland had few friends. As a sub-committee of the UFC, it was seen as incapable of offering impartial advice and the centrally-funded colleges as a group had no confidence in it.

The White Paper was warmly welcomed in Scotland as conferring an immediate and self-evident advantage. In the first place, it would create what many had campaigned for – a single funding council for higher education in Scotland. Henceforth, it would be possible for higher education in Scotland to be planned in a coherent way and in a way that took account of the distinctive features of the system. Besides, the ending of the binary distinction would put an end to the marginalisation of some institutions of higher education in Scotland. The incorporation of all of higher education within a single framework would not only enhance planning but also help to strengthen the international reputation of higher education in Scotland. Parallel legislation for England and Scotland gave effect to these changes and the Further and Higher Education (Scotland)

Act of 1992 provided the legal basis for a restructured higher education system in Scotland. In line with the legislation, the Scottish Higher Education Funding Council (SHEFC) was established and operated formally from 1 April 1993, with the responsibility for disbursing funds for teaching and research to all of Scotland's higher education institutions.

The following table demonstrates the extent of the changes that have occurred since the establishment of SHEFC. Column I gives the distribution of higher education institutions immediately prior to the establishment of the Council. Column II gives the position some 18 months after its establishment.

COLUMN I		COLUMN II	
Universities	8	Universities	13
Central Institutions	12	Central Institutions	5
Colleges of Education	5	Colleges of Education	3
Total	25	Total	21

The difference between the two columns is to be explained by the institutional redesignations and amalgamations following the 1992 legislation. Five of the former central institutions were designated as universities, and two of them merged with universities. In the college of education sphere, Jordanhill College of Education has become the Faculty of Education of Strathclyde University, and Craigie College of Education in Ayr has become the Faculty of Education of the University of Paisley. Of the eight non-university institutions, six have formed close academic collaboration with Scottish universities and one – Northern College – has a validating relationship with the Open University. It could have been predicted that the legislation would create a pattern of higher education in Scotland based on the universities and events since the Act have confirmed that prediction. At Moray House, in the light of the developments taking place more widely, a consultative exercise was carried out to test the extent of the desire to move towards a closer form of integration with Heriot-Watt University. A paper had been developed in the course of 1992 by the four Principals entitled *Towards a More Integrated University* and was widely discussed in all four institutions. The overwhelming view of Moray House was that the change would have meant a Model 2 type of association. However, the recommendations of the Principals' paper were not accepted and the Board of Governors, at its meeting in January 1993, decided to leave the arrangement with the university as previously agreed.

Despite variations in governance, then, it is reasonable now to speak of an integrated higher education system in Scotland. All 21 institutions have the same relationship with the Funding Council; they receive funds by the application of a widely understood formula; they are bound by the same Financial Memorandum; and are regulated consistently by SHEFC. In an academic sense, it is also reasonable to claim that common standards apply, for all 21 institutions are bound by the three main ways in which quality is guaranteed in the sector. The first of these involves research. Every three years all institutions, like all institutions in the United Kingdom, participate in the Research Assessment Exercise, which is an independent evaluation of the quality of research conducted in each of the institutions. The purpose of the exercise is to identify where the best research is undertaken and funds are allocated accordingly. The second concerns quality audit. Following the 1992 legislation, the Higher Education Quality Council has been established and one of the functions of that body is to visit institutions and to report on the mechanisms they have established for ensuring that high academic standards are enhanced and maintained. Again, the same standards apply across the whole of the United Kingdom. Finally, each of the Funding Councils has its own arrangements for quality assessment, the process by which, following visits to institutions to study the quality of teaching and learning on the ground and by applying a standard quality assessment framework, the quality of the teaching undertaken by institutions is assessed. Again, there are incentives for institutions which have a rating of 'excellent'.

It is clear, then, that institutions like Moray House have benefited from their association with universities and also by being part of a system in which they are judged according to the same criteria as university level institutions. There is no doubt that the continued application of these ways of testing quality will provide an incentive to enhance academic and professional standards still higher.

Conclusion

There is a striking contrast between the merger of Dunfermline College of Physical Education with Moray House and the establishment of the academic linkage between Moray House and Heriot-Watt University. The first of these was the result of ministerial decision. Neither institution sought the merger. It was the Secretary of State's response to the need to rationalise teacher education provision. On the other hand, the linkage with the University was self-originating. It was not a response to any kind of political pressure. Senior staff at Moray House, aware of the developments taking place nationally and of the danger that Moray House might not have a validating body and anxious to enhance the academic standing of Moray House, sought a relationship with Heriot-Watt University. That linkage anticipated some of the subsequent developments in higher education. Arguably, indeed, the Moray House breaching of the binary line may, itself, have been a factor in accelerating the developments that have helped to transform higher education in Scotland.

References

Kirk, G. 'The Future Context of Professional Education', in *Moray House and Professional Education 1835-1985*, edited by G. Kirk, Chapter 15, Scottish Academic Press, 1985.

Scottish Tertiary Education Advisory Council, *Future Strategy for Higher Education in Scotland*, HMSO, 1985.

Council for Tertiary Education in Scotland, *Review of Structure and Management*, Scottish Education Department, 1981.

National Audit Office, Report of the Controller and Auditor General, *Scottish Education Department: Control of Further Education Establishments*, HMSO, London, 1985.

Working Party on the centralisation of the training of physical education teachers and the merger of Dunfermline College of Physical Education with Moray House College of Education, Final Report, December 1986, Scottish Education Department.

Academic Validation in Public Sector Higher Education, HMSO, London, 1985, Command 9501.

White Paper, *Higher Education: Meeting the Challenge*, HMSO, London, 1987, Command 114.

Joint Working Party, *Proposals for Linkage*, Heriot-Watt University, 1990.

White Paper, *Higher Education: A New Framework*, HMSO, London, 1991, Command 1541.

2

Permanence, Policy and Partnership in Teacher Education

Margot Cameron-Jones

Introduction: Permanence

The contributors to this volume are asked to concentrate on change and development in the past decade. I shall do so. Perhaps heretically, however, I shall suggest that what has changed in teacher education in the period covered by this book might be of little real importance. I suggest this because, it seems to me, the task of teacher education always must be awesome in whatever period of history it is performed. In his inaugural lecture, which was more than a century ago, the first professor of Education at Edinburgh described (Morgan 1929) the task of the teacher educator as being:

> *To give the students of the subject an ideal and also a method but above all to inspire them with a sense of the infinite importance and delicacy of their task. He has to show them that they are not mere exacters of lessons, but trainers of the human spirit; and also how, animated by this large conception, they may, in teaching subjects, educate minds. He will expose the popular fallacy that the school master's work is a drudgery, and convince his students that it is a privilege.*

Everything worth aspiring to in this old description, I believe, applies today. There are some changes to be noted, however, with respect to our own times. These changes are to be seen in the nature of government policy about teacher education and in the arrangements for partnership between two key groups of teacher educators, namely university/college staff and school teachers. Both changes are discussed below.

Policy

Statements of government policy about teacher education are throughout the United Kingdom more assertive and more broad in their coverage now than they used to be. In England and Wales, and in Northern Ireland (DFE 1992, DFE 1993a, DFE 1993b, DENI 1993) two aspects of current policy are of particular importance. They are that student teachers must demonstrate a government-specified set of professional competences before they can qualify, and that their training must be heavily influenced by schools rather than dominated by the higher education institutions (HEIs). Both the matter and the manner of the policy statements which expressed these requirements have been strongly criticised and described as controversial (Becher 1994, Taylor 1994), sometimes bitterly so.

McNamara (1993) says that the expression of government policy in Scotland is more courteous and more reasonable in its style than elsewhere in the United Kingdom. He attributes to the existence in Scotland of the General Teaching Council a general gentling of Scottish educational affairs. Be that as it may, the two critical aspects of policy elsewhere in the United Kingdom which were described above, are established also here in Scotland. This has been the case since the Scottish Office Education Department published, in January 1993, after a period of consultation, its 'guidelines' for teacher education (SOED 1993). Since every course of teacher education in Scotland was to develop in accord with the 'guidelines', they were in effect requirements. In 12 pages they mandated, for all future courses of initial teacher training, the government's requirements.

The competences

Central to the SOED requirements is the statement of the professional competences in which all Scottish-trained teachers must be proficient. These competences are shown in summary in Figure 1 and are given in more detail in Figure 2 (Appendix). They are the same for all teachers, whatever their course, and so portray, for the primary and secondary training fields, 'the Scottish teacher' in terms of a set of what amounts to family resemblances across the whole profession. (This is an important point, since Scottish primary teachers are qualified to teach pupils from aged three years, and so the coverage of the competences, portraying as they do the nature of the teachers of pupils from three to 18 years, is very great.) In respect of the competences, both in the fact that they are stipulated by government and also in aspects of the way they are conceptualised, the similarity between the Scottish and the English/Welsh policy emphases is clear. There are however some differences.

One important difference is that the Scottish statement includes a broad, general definition of the term 'professional competences', saying that the term 'should be taken to refer to knowledge, understanding, critical thinking and positive attitudes, as well as to practical skills'. The English/ Welsh statements, in contrast, do not put 'critical thinking' in the foreground in a similarly firm explicit way.

The role of the schools

The role of the schools is also central to the Scottish guidelines, but again there are some differences between the Scottish statement and other ones in Britain. For example, a recent English/Welsh paper (DFE 1993b) proposed that schools 'should be able, if they wish, to play the leading role in planning and providing courses'. No suggestion of such leadership of teacher education by the schools has been proposed for Scotland. However, in Scotland the respective roles of school and HEI certainly are required to be defined and, with regard to students' development of particular areas of competence, authority is certainly accorded to the schools. For instance, the guidelines say that students' 'particular skills in dealing with class management and curriculum' are 'best developed in the partner schools'.

The theme of partnership between HEIs and schools recurs throughout the guidelines: they require that all courses of teacher education will rest on a partnership between the HEI and schools, with school teachers having a formal role in the design and conduct of courses, and in the assessment of students; and that during their course students will spend specified lengths of time in schools (rather than in the HEIs). For all students, the amount of time to be spent in schools is appreciable. For example, if students train as primary teachers they spend at least a quarter of their course in schools if they are on the four-year undergraduate course, and at least a half if they are on the graduate course.

The government's stance about initial teacher training in this country accordingly is clear. It includes the requirement that schools and HEIs must share the responsibility for initial teacher training, on the basis of a clear partnership between them. What kind of partnership exists at present on which to build a co-operative future of that kind?

Partnership

The present partnership in initial teacher training is one in which students apply for entry to initial teacher training to the HEI, enrol for their course at the HEI and qualify as teachers by means of certification by and graduation from the HEI. Described like that, the balance of the partnership may seem very much in favour of the HEI. In fact, however, school teachers play a role in every HEI's acceptance of students on every course of training and, as has been outlined above, a considerable amount of student training and assessment takes place not in the HEIs at all, but during student placement with teachers in the schools. Accordingly, the teachers of Scotland have a formidable presence in every student's professional formation and a powerful say in every student's final qualification to enter their profession.

The role of school teachers in Scottish teacher education not only has a high reputation now but also has a reputable history. In addition, it is an explicit part (SED 1986) of the Scottish teacher's life, since the formal definition of their job includes the duty to:

> *contribute to the professional development of colleagues including probationary and student teachers.*

In recent years, the level of recognition of the role of school teachers in student teacher training has been raised for two reasons. The first is policy, and that has been outlined above. The second is scholarship, and that will be outlined below.

Scholars' respect for practitioner knowledge

Respect for practitioner knowledge is not new among scholars based in HEIs. For more than a decade the literature in the field of teacher education (e.g. Hoyle 1982, Hirst 1982) has pointed out that teachers' knowledge, and teachers' ways of using what they know, has a character of its own which is different from the academic knowledge which is created and sustained by scholars in the HEIs.

Recent work (Brown and McIntyre 1993) on practitioner knowledge supports the claim that it is rich, practical and fruitful in itself and also full of potential as an influence on the development of students. Calderhead (1991) in claiming for teachers' knowledge a place in the curriculum of student teachers' alongside 'book knowledge', pointed out that 'Learning to teach is different from other forms of learning in academic life. Teacher education has always sat uneasily in Higher Education institutions, partly because it does not involve an emphasis on the abstract 'book knowledge' of traditional disciplines'. Hagger *et al* (1993) also support the view that the knowledge base of teachers enables them to make a contribution to student training which is not only valuable in itself but is also different from the contribution which can be made by staff located in the HEIs. They say:

The expertise of experienced teachers is strikingly different in nature from the academic knowledge which can be offered by universities and colleges. Whereas the former is practical, contextualised, implicit in teachers' practice and varies with the individual, the latter is often idealised, is necessarily generalised across contexts and aims to be as explicit and as objective as possible.

Other scholars in recent times (e.g. Edwards 1992a, 1992b) have come increasingly to share this view. They advance the notion of 'complementarity' as the basis of the partnership in teacher education. The assumption they make, therefore, is that neither schools nor HEIs alone can make a student's education as a teacher whole and complete but that, rather, the two should complement each other, each one contributing its own distinctive knowledge and authority to the partnership.

To what degree does this kind of partnership exist today?

Current evidence about partnership

(i) Students' views

Much of the research on students' views of college/school partnership in recent times has been done at Moray House.

For example, in the year preceding the publication of the SOED guidelines, the national pilot study of the new arrangements for initial teacher training (Cameron-Jones and O'Hara 1993) took place with over 200 students on the PGCE Secondary course at Moray House. (The PGCE Secondary course is a one-year teacher training for university graduates to teach in secondary schools – i.e. to teach pupils aged 12 to 18 years.) The pilot study was concerned with course arrangements which were somewhat similar to those which were subsequently outlined under the new SOED guidelines (SOED 1993). The pilot study showed the students expecting at the start of their course, and at the end of their course feeling that they had indeed experienced, greater influence from schools than from the college on their professional development. In addition, the sub-group of 'experimental' students who had been given intensified contact with schools and teachers (through spending additional time in schools, and being provided with specially-trained mentors who were members of the staffs of the schools) did rather better on, and felt somewhat happier about, the course than did the other students.

Not until the 1993-4 courses, however, could there be investigation of student views in the context of a more 'normal' rather than a 'special pilot' situation. It is interesting to note, therefore, that the students who enrolled on the PGCE Secondary course of 1993-4 had clear expectations of a partnership between Moray House and schools (Cameron-Jones and O'Hara 1994a). Two hundred and fifty students enrolled on that course. Two hundred and forty-six of them filled in a questionnaire about what they expected to experience during the course with respect to learning, getting help with, being assessed on and having demands made in relation to the competences shown in Figure 1.

Did they expect during the course to be influenced in the main by schools, in the main by Moray House or in the main by both parties equally? Table 1 (Appendix) summarises the findings from the questionnaire in order to provide an answer to this question. It shows most students expecting the main influence on them to reflect a partnership of college and school. However, where one party (rather than both together) was expected to predominate in influence, Table 1 shows that this one party was more frequently expected to be the school, rather than the college. Further, Table 1 shows the influence of the school being expected to be particularly strong on students' development of competence in the classroom; and Table 2 (Appendix) shows that when the students were asked to rank the competences for their anticipated difficulty, the classroom competences were expected by the students to be among the harder competences to learn.

The evidence is, then, that students from the moment they enrolled on their course had high expectations of the experience they would have while they were with teachers in the schools, especially with respect to some of the things which the students thought would be very difficult to learn. Importantly, subsequent research with the same students at the end of their course (Cameron-Jones and O'Hara 1994c) showed that the students felt that their high expectations of the teachers had been fulfilled. It is understandable therefore (and this will be discussed below), since Scottish-trained students spend so much training time in schools, that when students finally graduate, their potential employers value very highly the information about how students perform while they are in schools. The research we have done on that is now discussed over.

(ii) What employers want to read in the students' final
reports when they qualify as teachers

When students qualify as teachers and apply for jobs, their
potential employers frequently ask their training institutions for
reports about them. In Scotland, such reports have a standard
format and include a space in which comments on the students
can be written by the staff of the HEIs. Previous research across
Scotland showed in 1990 however (Cameron-Jones and O'Hara
1990) that when higher education staff used this space to write
comment on their students, the comments they wrote were not
found helpful by the students' potential employers. An
experimental Scottish study (Cameron-Jones and O'Hara 1994b)
was carried out from Moray House in the context of the reporting
system when it was revised in 1993 to bring it into line with the
competences specified in the newly-published SOED guidelines
(SOED 1993). In the study, two samples of Scottish respondents
passed judgment on what kind of comments should appear in
students' final reports in order to make the comment most helpful
to employers. The respondents were presented with simulated
student reports containing three different kinds of comments, all
positive, which genuinely had been written in real reports about
real students by the staffs of all the Scottish HEIs. One kind of
comment was predictive, saying how the student might develop
once employed as a teacher. One kind was based on general
evidence about what the student had done on the course of
training. The last kind was based specifically on what the student
had done while on placement in schools. (An example of this
kind of comment was: 'she was commended by schools during
every placement for her commitment, enthusiasm and willingness
to participate fully in the whole life of the school.') As is shown
in Tables III and IV (Appendix) it was the last kind of comment
which was valued most. It was the kind most frequently chosen
by both samples of respondents as being 'the Most Helpful' kind
to have on students' Final Reports when the students graduated
and applied to employers for jobs as teachers.

In terms of emphasising the importance of the schools' part in teacher
education, these findings are in line with the students' expectations,
reported above. From course start to course completion, then, various
different pieces of research done from Moray House give evidence of
high value being placed on the role of schools in the field of teacher

education and on what students show they can do in schools while they are being trained by school teachers.

This is important since, as was mentioned earlier, the formal responsibilities of the HEIs in the field of teacher education are very great, and seem formally much greater than those of the partner schools. It is the HEIs who must select, enrol, certificate and qualify young teachers and who must issue the crucial, first reports to their would-be employers. Expressed like that, the roles of schools and teachers seem somewhat marginal. The reality, however, disconfirms that view. Schools are not by any means seen as the junior or lesser partners in teacher education, either in the eyes of students or in the eyes of their future employers. The researches I have cited make that very clear.

Discussion – permanence, policy and partnership

To conclude; recent policy changes and recent research studies have confirmed initial teacher education as the sphere of influence of schools and HEIs in partnership, rather than as the exclusive satrapy of the HEIs. Some academics (e.g. Edwards 1992b) accept that our field should, in line with this conception, rest complementarily on 'a division of labour' between two training partners, namely the HEIs and schools. In the eyes of other academics, however, there is no doubt, the current heavy emphasis on the schools' side of the partnership can only threaten in a fundamental way the intellectual base of their field. Anxiety on this score is evident throughout the literature of the field at present, even though recognition of the role of schools in initial teacher education, and suggestions about the need to rethink the nature and balance of school/HEI partnership accordingly, are by no means new. Half a century ago, for example, the McNair report (Board of Education 1944) discussed the fact that if practising teachers were to have a desirably greater influence in initial teacher training, the HEIs would have to 'relinquish a measure of responsibility in the training of their students'. Despite this idea's long-standing history, however, it has failed to win complete acceptance. Goodson (1993) for example is not only gloomy in noting the global tendency for more teacher education to become more school-based nowadays but scathing in his observation that:

> *The hasty embrace of 'practical' and 'field-based' teacher education*
> *has gone further and faster in Britain than elsewhere.*

Rather differently, Gardner (1992) takes a long, historical perspective on the issue. He sees a 'reforming pendulum' influencing initial teacher training and notes its swing towards the schools in the 19th century and its swing towards the HEIs in the early 20th. Now, he says, the reforming pendulum is swinging once again, and maybe, he hints, too far in favour of the schools. If not anxiety, certainly perplexity, about today's position has underpinned the recent writing also of other, thoughtful teacher educators (e.g. Hartley 1993) including those who believe in a partnership based on 'complementarity' but feel that complementarity itself is jeopordised by a lack of government understanding of the contribution of the HEIs (Edwards 1994).

In Scotland, however, and some reasons for this have been given in this chapter, the relationship between the HEIs and schools with respect to teacher training continues to be one predominantly influenced by conceptions of professionalism rather than eroded by anxieties of the kind discussed above. Certainly, our field in the 1990s has felt disequilibrium as a result of central government's interventionist policies with respect to teacher training. Further, because of new arrangements in the funding base and the financial management of HEIs and schools, and in the structure of local government, our field has been affected by successively changing uncertainties concerning the politics and financing of our work. Despite these things, however, strongly held conceptions of professionalism still underpin the culture of Scottish teacher education, still drive our college's definition of itself today and still contribute to the relationships between our college and its partner schools.

That is why, although this chapter has situated Moray House and its work within what sometimes feels like a context in ferment, I can nonetheless suggest that little of fundamental importance might have changed. I am saying, you see, that what ultimately matters in teacher education is not who 'does' it, or who 'owns' it or even what governments might say about it as they come and go. These things are certainly important. But it is more important to have teacher educators, whether they are HEI staff or school staff, who have a large conception of their task; and are dedicated to their students and the field. Those things we have.

This chapter, therefore, while acknowledging major changes in our political, financial and administrative contexts, maintains that things of permanent value continue, rightly, to be present in our field.

Appendix

Figure 1

The competences

1. Competences relating to the subject and content of teaching
   Competences relating to the classroom
2. Communication
3. Methodology
4. Management
5. Assessment
6. Competences relating to the school
7. Competences relating to the profession

Figure 2

Details of the competences

1. **SUBJECT AND CONTENT OF TEACHING**
   Demonstrate a wide knowledge of curriculum content
   Plan, including coherent teaching programmes and lessons within them
   Present subject content appropriately
   Justify what is taught from knowledge and understanding of the learning process

   THE CLASSROOM
2. **Communication**
   Present what is taught clearly and in a stimulating manner
   Question effectively and support discussion

3. **Methodology**
   Employ a range of teaching strategies
   Identify whole class, group, pair or individual teaching opportunities
   Create contexts in which pupils can learn

Set expectations which make appropriate demands on pupils
Identify and respond to the special educational needs of all pupils
Take cultural differences into account
Encourage pupils to be responsible for their own learning
Select and use a wide variety of resources
Evaluate and justify methodology being used

4. **Management**
   Create and maintain a purposeful, orderly and safe environment of
   learning
   Manage pupil behaviour
   Sustain pupil interest and motivation
   Evaluate own classroom management

5. **Assessment**
   Understand the principles of assessment
   Assess quality of pupils' learning against relevant national standards
   Assess and record progress
   Provide regular feedback to pupils
   Use assessment to evaluate and improve teaching

6. **THE SCHOOL**
   Show knowledge of school management, policies and plans in the
   context of the educational system
   Know how to discuss pupil progress with parents
   Know how to communicate with colleagues, other professionals and
   members of the community
   Know how to use help and expertise within the school
   Be aware of and contribute to cross-curricular aspects of school work
   Be able to contribute to extra-curricular activities

7. **PROFESSIONALISM**
   Have a working knowledge of pastoral and contractual responsibilities
   Be able to make an evaluation of own professional progress
   Demonstrate commitment to the values of the profession including:
   > the job and those affected by it
   > professional development
   > collaboration to promote pupil achievement
   > the well-being of pupils
   > the school and its community
   > views of fairness and equality

Table I

STUDENTS' EXPECTATIONS (%) OF INFLUENCE ON THEIR EDUCATION AS TEACHERS (n = 246 students from a class of 250), PRESENTED IN TERMS OF THE 7 COMPETENCES (CO = Influence expected Mainly from College, SC = Mainly from Schools, BO = from Both Equally).

THE 7 COMPETENCES	STUDENTS' EXPECTATIONS OF INFLUENCE ON THEM DURING THEIR YEAR OF TRAINING		
	CO	SC	BO
1. Subject and content of Teaching The Classroom	26	26	47
2. Communication	3	58	30
3. Methodology	28	19	54
4. Management	3	57	39
5. Assessment	19	28	53
6. The School	28	31	41
7. Professionalism	36	9	54
TOTAL	**23**	**32**	**45**

Table II

STUDENTS' EXPECTATIONS (mean ranks) OF THE COMPETENCES THEY WOULD FIND EASIER AND HARDER TO LEARN DURING THEIR COURSE, 1 BEING THE EASIEST TO LEARN AND 7 BEING THE HARDEST.

(n = 156 usable replies)

THE 7 COMPETENCES	MEAN RANK	OVERALL RANK
1. Subject and content of Teaching The Classroom	2.2	1
2. Communication	4.1	4
3. Methodology	4.2	5
4. Management	5.8	7
5. Assessment	5.3	6
6. The School	2.9	2
7. Professionalism	3.4	3

Table III

Results from the first group of respondents (63 teacher employers and trainers).
Comments seen as the most helpful ones to have on students' Final Reports.

CATEGORY OF COMMENTS	PERCENTAGE OF CHOICES AS 'THE MOST HELPFUL' COMMENTS
Comments resting on school-based evidence	41%
Comments resting on general evidence	35%
Predictive comments	24%

Table IV

Results from the second group of respondents (51 HEI staff).
Comments seen as the most helpful ones to have on students' Final Reports.

CATEGORY OF COMMENTS	PERCENTAGE OF CHOICES AS 'THE MOST HELPFUL' COMMENTS
Comments resting on school-based evidence	49%
Comments resting on general evidence	32%
Predictive comments	19%

References

Becher, T. (1994). Freedom and Accountability in Professional Curricula in *Governments and Professional Education*, Buckingham, Society for Research into Higher Education and Open University Press.

Board of Education (1944). *Teachers and Youth Leaders (The McNair Report)* London, HMSO.

Brown, S. and McIntyre, D. (1993). *Making Sense of Teaching*, Buckingham, Open University Press.

Calderhead, J. (1991). The Nature and Growth of Knowledge in Teaching, *Teaching and Teacher Education*, 7, 5/6, 531-535.

Cameron-Jones, M. and O'Hara, P. (1990). Getting the Measure of New Teachers in Scotland: Does the System Work? *Scottish Educational Review*, 22, 38-44.

Cameron-Jones, M. and O'Hara, P. (1993). *The Scottish Pilot PGCE (Secondary) Course 1992-1993*, Edinburgh, Moray House Institute/Heriot-Watt mimeo.

Cameron-Jones, M. and O'Hara, P. (1994a). *Pressures on the Curriculum of Teacher Education*, Scottish Educational Review, 26, 134-142.

Cameron-Jones, M. and O'Hara, P. (1994b). What Employers Want to Read About New Teachers, *Journal of Education for Teaching*, 20, 203-214.

Cameron-Jones, M. and O'Hara, P. (1994c). *The Second Year (1993-4) of the Scottish Pilot PGCE (Secondary) Course*, Edinburgh, Moray House Institute/Heriot-Watt mimeo.

DFE (1992). *Circular 9/92 and Circular 35/92 Initial Teacher Training (Secondary Phase)*, London, Department for Education.

DFE (1993a). *Circular 14.93 The Initial Training of Primary School Teachers: New Criteria for Courses*, London, Department for Education.

DFE (1993b). *The Government's Proposals for the Reform of Initial Teacher Training*, London, Department for Education.

DENI (1993). *Review of Initial Teacher Training (ITT) in Northern Ireland*, Belfast, Department of Education Northern Ireland.

Edwards, T. (1992a). *Change and Reform in Initial Teacher Education* NCE Briefing No. 9, National Commission on Education, London, Paul Hamlyn.

Edwards, T. (1992b). Issues and Challenges in Initial Teacher Education, *Cambridge Journal of Education*, 22, 283-291.

Edwards, T. (1994). The Universities Council for the Education of Teachers: defending an interest or fighting a course? *Journal of Education for Teaching*, 20, 143-152.

Gardner, P. (1993). The Early History of School-Based Teacher Training in D. McIntyre et al (Ed). *Mentoring: Perspectives on School-Based Teacher Education*, London, Kogan Page.

Goodson, I. F. (1993). Forms of Knowledge and Teacher Education, International Analyses of Teacher Education, Special Issue of *Journal of Education for Teaching*, 19, 217-229.

Hagger, H., Burn, K. and McIntyre, D. (1993). *The School Mentor Handbook*, London, Kogan Page.

Hartley, D. (1993). Confusion in Teacher Education: a postmodern condition? International Analysis of Teacher Education, Special Issue of *Journal of Education for Teaching*, 19, 83-93.

Hirst, P. H. (1982). Professional Authority: Its Foundations and Limits, *British Journal of Educational Studies*, 30, 172-182.

Hoyle, E. (1982). The Professionalisation of Teachers: A Paradox, *British Journal of Educational Studies*, 30, 161-171.

McNamara, D. (1993). Towards Re-establishing the Professional Authority and Expertise of Teacher Educators and Teachers, *International Analysis of Teacher Education*, Special Issue of *Journal of Education for Teaching* 19, 277-291.

Morgan, A. (1929). *Makers of Scottish Education*, London Longmans.

SED, Scottish Education Department (1986). *Committee of Inquiry Report into the pay and conditions of service of school teachers in Scotland*, Edinburgh, Her Majesty's Stationery Office.

SOED, Scottish Office Education Department (1993). *Guidelines for Teacher Training Courses*, Scottish Office Education Department, Edinburgh, Her Majesty's Stationery Office.

Taylor, Sir W. (1994). Teacher Education: Backstage to Centre Stage in T. Becher, (Ed.) *Governments and Professional Education* Buckingham, The Society for Research into Higher Education and Open University Press.

3

The Scottish Centre for Physical Education, Movement and Leisure Studies

David M. Bayman

The Creation of the Centre

In 1985, when Moray House was celebrating its 150th anniversary, Dunfermline College of Physical Education (DCPE) was providing specialist courses for physical education teachers and recreation/leisure professionals at Cramond in Edinburgh. 'Dunf' (or 'Dumf'), as it was known to its students and alumni, was founded in 1905 with the help of the Carnegie Dunfermline Trust. Originally based in Dunfermline, it moved twice, initially to Aberdeen, and finally to new custom-built premises in Edinburgh in 1966.[1] As a small college of approximately 500 students, DCPE had mounted a vigorous and successful campaign against government proposals to close it or to merge it, possibly with another Scottish college. At that time, unlike some other colleges, it had a full complement of students and was allowed to continue when, in 1981, the college system was reduced from ten to seven colleges, with the closure of Hamilton and Callendar Park, and with the merger of Craiglockhart and Notre Dame to create the new St Andrew's College of Education.

However, with the continuation of the falling demand for physical education teachers during the eighties, two issues needed to be addressed. Firstly, although DCPE had at one time accepted both male and female students, training in physical education on a single-sex basis in Scotland had been established with the opening of the Scottish School of Physical Education at Jordanhill College in the 1920's. With an increase in the teaching of mixed classes in schools it seemed, to some, illogical and inconsistent that male physical education teachers were still being trained in Glasgow and their female counterparts in Edinburgh. Secondly, small units were increasingly under attack on both economic and educational grounds. DCPE had moved into the recreation/leisure field but proposals to diversify further had not found favour with SED, who viewed the areas into which DCPE proposed to move as being the territory of the central institutions. The situation was resolved by SED's decision in 1986, which was implemented in April 1987, that all Scottish physical education teachers would in future be trained in Edinburgh and that the centre for this training would merge with Moray House, although remaining at the Cramond premises.

This merger produced a range of consequences and developments. One of the most immediate and public matters concerned the title of the merged institutions. This was eventually enshrined in legislation as 'Moray House College of Education (incorporating the Scottish Centre for Physical Education Movement and Leisure Studies)'. This unwieldy title reflected a long-standing debate on the nature and standing of degrees in physical education and related areas. The title recognised the need to establish and publicly acknowledge the existence of a national centre for these areas of study to the satisfaction of all parties.

The new SCOPEMALS, an integral feature of the enlarged Moray House, inherited a range of courses at undergraduate and postgraduate levels: the BEd Degree and Honours Degree in Physical Education, the BA Degree and Honours Degree in Recreation, the Postgraduate Diploma in Recreation and Leisure Practice, and the Diploma in Sports Coaching. In the aftermath of the restructuring of colleges of education by the Secretary of State in the light of the Scottish Tertiary Education Advisory Council (STEAC) Report[2], the BEd Physical Education received its first mixed intake of 80 students, 28 males and 52 females, in 1987, thereby producing a total undergraduate cohort in excess of 300 on what was the only specialist Physical Education course in Scotland. The BA Recreation provided an undergraduate course of study and initial training for those intending to make a professional career in the rapidly expanding leisure and recreation industries. Recruitment was from throughout the UK and involved an initial intake of 25 students, resulting in total course numbers of approximately 100. Alongside this undergraduate provision for almost 400 students, the two postgraduate awards in Recreation and Leisure Practice and Sports Coaching attracted a small group of 14 students.

In addition to these programmes, the new centre offered at the time of its establishment four other types of provision. Firstly, it provided a range of part-time in-service courses for teachers of physical education, dance, movement and outdoor education, either on the Cramond Campus or on an outreach basis in schools and authorities throughout Scotland. Secondly, it had established a specialist centre to create opportunities for professional collaboration and development in sports coaching. The National Coaching Centre (NCC), which was established in 1983, complemented the Diploma in Sports Coaching. In 1984, on the basis of financial assistance from the Scottish Sports Council, NCC became one of fourteen such centres operating in the UK supported by joint funding from national sports bodies. Thirdly, a research base, the Centre for Leisure Research, had been established to foster and support a range of research activities and developments in leisure and recreation and involved funded and contract research activities. Finally, the Community Activities Programme (CAP) had been successfully established in 1976 and had developed impressively by utilising the expertise and resources of the college and making these available to the local community and to specialist groups throughout the country. The programme was marketed nationally and internationally and included residential and non-residential conferences on the Cramond Campus.

The amalgamation provided an opportunity for the academic resources required to underpin the total institutional programme of Moray House College to be re-assessed and one of the major changes arising from the merger involved the reduction of the 32 academic departments on the Holyrood Campus and six Cramond-based departments to 14, of which three constituted the new centre at Cramond. These were the Department of Physical Education, the Department of Movement Studies, and the Department of Leisure Studies. In total, the three departments involved over 40 academic staff, together with the significant number of support staff associated with the services provided on the Cramond Campus.

The merger brought together two established and respected institutions in Scottish higher education, both of which had strong professional reputations. The established role and international standing of Moray House in primary and secondary teacher education combined with the centre of excellence status DCPE had attained, throughout Scotland and the UK as well as abroad, in women's physical education, movement, dance and outdoor education and its emerging status in related fields of recreation, leisure and sport. The merger of the two institutions and the creation of the national centre for the specialist activities of physical education, movement and leisure studies created an appropriate context for development in these areas of academic and professional work.

Undergraduate Course Developments

The validation of the BEd/BEd (Hons) Physical Education and BA/BA (Hons) Recreation degrees by CNAA in 1988 provided a firm foundation for undergraduate work at SCOPEMALS in the latter half of the eighties. From the 1988 quota of 80 per annum for the Physical Education degree, numbers rose to 96 in 1991 and have been progressively reduced by the Scottish Office Education Department (SOED) to 80 by 1994 to reflect the changing needs of schools in Scotland.

Set against the significant changes which have occurred in teacher education course provision elsewhere in the UK during the last decade, the nature and level of provision in Scotland has been far less dramatically affected. In relation to specialist physical education course provision in England and Wales, there was a substantial reduction from over 50 institutions involved in non-specialist and specialist physical education course provision in the eighties to around 15 institutions providing DES-approved specialist teacher education courses in physical education by the early nineties.[3] The approach to specialist provision in Scotland, through SCOPEMALS, has been more stable and less damaging to the physical education profession than elsewhere in the UK and the Scottish Centre has fulfilled an important role in maintaining the existence of the four-year specialist course of training in Physical Education at a time when this type of specialist provision is in decline elsewhere in Britain. The attractiveness of the Cramond-based physical education course is clearly evident in the application rate: in 1994 in excess of seven qualified applicants applied for each place, thus ensuring that the quality of the intake is extremely high.

The intake to the BA Recreation course has expanded from its initial intake of 25 to over 40 in 1994 to produce a total cohort of about 140 students compared to less than 100 in 1987. With its vocational, as well as academic dimension, the Recreation course throughout the decade has provided a broadly-based approach to studies in this area. Applications for the increasing number of places available during the nineties have been on a strongly competitive basis, with a marked increased in mature students during this period. In 1993, 41 per cent of successful applicants for the course were over 24 years of age. Graduates obtaining the award are predominantly employed in the developing area of leisure, recreation and leisure management and administration.[4]

These two degrees provided an important base for undergraduate studies at the Scottish Centre but opportunities to expand further were controlled by SOED until 1993. On the establishment of the Scottish Higher Education Funding Council (SHEFC) and the introduction of new funding arrangements, institutions assumed increased responsibilities in relation to student numbers for some of their courses, particularly in areas other than teacher education. Although strict controls on overall student numbers are maintained, it has proved possible for the Scottish Centre to establish an additional undergraduate degree course in 1994 – a BSc in Applied Sport Sciences. This widening of the undergraduate provision, involving a further intake of 21 students in the first year, enables the selection of high calibre students with strong academic background and specialised sporting experience and/or skills in this new academic area to be added to the highly qualified entrants selected for the other two undergraduate degree programmes.

Taken together, these three undergraduate programmes offer academic opportunities for specialised study in physical education, recreation, sport, the arts, countryside studies, exercise and health. Access to these opportunities is highly competitive. The quality of the intake of around 150 students per year, and the concentration of relevant studies in carefully constructed programmes, creates an entirely appropriate ethos for a national centre.

Postgraduate Developments

One of the indications of the standing of prestigious institutions in a particular subject or academic area is the portfolio of course provision which is available for postgraduate study. The national centre for physical education, movement and leisure studies in Scotland at the time of its establishment had limited postgraduate opportunities, with only two diploma programmes in operation and attracting fewer than 20 students a year. Over the past decade, Moray House has been strongly committed to the substantial expansion of postgraduate opportunities. Consequently, following the successful validation of the first master's degree in Leisure in Scotland by SCOPEMALS in 1990, involving the MA/Postgraduate Diploma in Leisure Policy and Practice, a rolling programme of development of specialist masters' degrees has operated. The MSc/ Postgraduate Diploma in Coaching Studies was introduced in 1991, the only course of its kind in the UK. Other postgraduate programmes developed by SCOPEMALS include postgraduate and master's degree opportunities in Cultural Services Management, Cultural Policy and Management, Exercise and Health Sciences, and Dance. Moreover, the modules which make up these awards form part of a total institutional set in excess of 300, thus offering a significant degree of choice in the combination of studies for practising professionals.

Postgraduate provision at SCOPEMALS by 1994 involved over 125 students and appears likely to continue to increase in the future. Some of these courses qualify for bursaries from the SOED and DES or from national organisations including the Scottish Physical Recreation Trust Fund, administered by the Scottish Sports Council. The bursary provision for students at the Scottish Centre is expected to increase. Moreover, additional students from UK, Europe and other overseas countries also participate in the postgraduate programme. An increasing number of students from overseas universities, including those at Leuven, Strasbourg and Lyon, are opting to take modules from the MHIE postgraduate programme. Additionally, some overseas students undertake parts of their research degree studies at the Scottish Centre. This portfolio of courses, which is recruiting successfully and impressively from Scotland, the United Kingdom and abroad, represents a major development for the institution and has significantly strengthened the national centre role and reputation of SCOPEMALS.

Of course, the extension of postgraduate opportunities both requires and stimulates an increased academic environment in which research flourishes. An increased number of staff have possessed further academic qualifications with five staff (18 per cent) holding or currently awaiting the award of doctorates. Expertise in selected scientific disciplines has been strengthened, thereby reflecting the increasing numbers of students selecting to study these perspectives. Research forms an increasingly important feature of academic staff work and is supported in many instances by the appointment of research or graduate assistants. The developing research strength of the new Department was reflected in the appointment of the first Chair at the Scottish Centre in 1994 in the field of Leisure and Recreation. All of these developments have been strengthened through the academic links with Heriot-Watt University.

The development of research, in turn, as well as an expanding range of undergraduate and postgraduate opportunities, requires appropriate facilities. However, facility provision on the Cramond Campus during the past decade has been mixed. Despite strenuous efforts to obtain funding for enhanced indoor games facilities and other requirements, support from SOED has not been forthcoming. However, an all-weather floodlight area, which provides an excellent facility principally for hockey, has been established. In addition, there has been up-grading of other facilities. A Sports Science Laboratory has been created, providing a significantly enhanced facility for scientific studies in physical education, sport and outdoor activities. The creation of a Dance Resource Centre, a Motor Learning Laboratory, a new Student Computer Area, and a comprehensive refurbishment of lecture theatres and other study areas have provided improved facilities for students on courses and for staff involvement in research. Nevertheless, there remains an urgent need for substantial capital investment in the Cramond Campus facilities. A comprehensive estates strategy has been developed by the Institute and provision has been made to secure the necessary investment in the Cramond Campus. In the meantime, the launch of a network of specialist sports colleges represents a complementary avenue of development. The intention is to improve standards for elite sports people in Scotland and, in the initiative by the Sports Council, reference is made to facilities at Moray House in Edinburgh which '. . . already fill some of the functions of a sports college. The new scheme would harness work which is being done at present and tie in added elements of sports science, sports medicine, as well as specialist skills coaching.'[5] Joint initiatives with other agencies involved in sport in Scotland would offer an important supplementary source of resource development for the Scottish Centre in future alongside the institutional commitment already being made.

Professional Collaboration

One of the central features of academic and professional work undertaken at MHIE has been a strong commitment to fostering and strengthening links with professionals in a variety of different settings. Close and sustained working relationships with agencies, organisations and individuals in Leisure and Recreation have been central to the implementing of the BA and MA courses in Recreation and Leisure. The opinions and advice of leisure professionals have been important in the validation and re-validation of courses during the period under review, while student placement on undergraduate courses in a wide range of organisations and agencies reflects the extent and standing of the professional collaboration that has been developed.

In the same way, strong collaborative relationships have been developed in the field of physical education. Curriculum initiatives in physical education in Scotland, as illustrated by developments in Standard Grade Physical Education in the eighties and Higher Grade Physical Education in the nineties, have enabled a substantial number of academic staff to make significant contributions to these major curricular initiatives. Either as development officers, chairs and members of key development groups, authors of key texts and documents, staff have been involved in influential and important curricular initiatives and have played a significant role in these developments. Currently, the 5-14 national programme, particularly its Expressive Arts component, and the developments relating to the reform of upper secondary education known as the 'Higher Still' initiative, will continue this important partnership with field professionals at national level. Similar developments are taking place in Outdoor Education, Dance, and Coaching Studies.

International Initiatives and Developments

The Scottish Centre has made a significant contribution to the development of academic links and exchanges with institutions overseas, which has been actively promoted by MHIE since the beginning of the nineties. Through a range of funding schemes including ERASMUS, TEMPUS and SOCRATES, an increasing number of staff and students from the Scottish Centre and from higher education institutions abroad have been involved in visits, exchanges and various forms of academic and professional collaboration. The range of collaborative schemes includes programmes with universities in Belgium, Finland, France, Germany, Greece, Holland, Portugal and Spain. Over 40 students each year are involved in visits to partner institutions for periods varying from a number of days to a complete academic year. Students visiting the Scottish Centre identify the undergraduate or postgraduate modules on which they wish to enrol during their visit, with some also engaging in placement attachments involving schools and/or leisure or recreation centres in Scotland. Some research students visit SCOPEMALS to access specialised expertise or facilities. For their part, students from the Scottish Centre similarly undertake periods of study of varying lengths abroad with some completing a full academic year at a partner institution abroad. Some Cramond students are able to undertake one of their school placements in such countries as Canada and Switzerland.

Through these various forms of international activity, the Scottish Centre has ensured that it forms part of a network of higher education institutions with a specialised interest in areas of study such as sport, dance, exercise, physical education, and health. By participating in these networks, staff engagement in research and consultancy activity is fostered.

The Institutional Context

Prior to the establishment of the Centre, Dunfermline College of Physical Education had already embarked on a number of activities which helped to diversify the range of activities undertaken, as well as to enrich the academic life of the institution. Reference has already been made to the Centre for Leisure Research. Over the period since the merger, that centre has strengthened its standing as a leading research establishment in the UK. Another feature of the pre-merger days – the Community Activities Programme – has been also been developed and now provides a wide range of opportunities for recreation and informal education for more than 5,000 people in the course of a single year.

Reference has also been made to the National Coaching Centre (NCC). As the work of the Centre has developed, a number of distinctive benefits to the institution have become apparent. Resource provision has been enhanced on the Cramond Campus through the funding of laboratory equipment by the Scottish Sports Council to enable the NCC to strengthen its work. Research and development work undertaken by NCC staff regularly produces significant research income for the institution, and staff development activities through courses, conferences, and sports science monitoring programme undertaken by the NCC have enriched the environment provided by the Centre. Through the work undertaken by the co-ordinator, John Lyle, the four full-time staff and the part-time director, the NCC has become recognised as one of the largest and most pro-active and successful of such centres in the UK. Its influence on coaching and coach education in Scotland has been considerable.

A further example of centre development involves the Sports Medicine Centre (SMC). The centre was established to deal with the specialist medical needs of students on courses with a substantial physical component. SMC currently aims to provide an early and appropriate diagnostic and therapeutic service to all students in MHIE who have soft tissue sporting injuries. Dr McSwan, the Medical Officer, and her physiotherapist colleague, Liz Mendel, also provide diagnostic and medical services for many athletes and sports people in Scotland and beyond. As a result, they hold many honorary positions with Scottish and UK sports bodies and their expertise is highly regarded.

During the 1991-92 academic year an additional centre, the National Centre for Play (NCP), was added to those already operating on the Cramond Campus. This unit, which relocated from the Holyrood Campus, provided a range of services for groups involved in the promotion and development of play and playwork. Through the dissemination of information bulletins, news sheets and the organisation of conferences, NCP has established an important role in the network which operates in play and its position has been recognised through grant from the Scottish Office. NCP has been influential in the development of standards of training, performance and qualifications appropriate to this area, including the provision of a postgraduate award in Playwork. In these ways, NCP has made an important contribution to the professionalisation of playwork. Moreover, the existence of NCP has offered opportunities for students on a range of courses at Moray

House to gain first-hand experience of some of the developments occurring in Scotland, the UK and selected European countries.

Although not formally established as a Centre, the area of Exercise, Health and Fitness has undergone a decade of significant development. This work originated in 1978 when DCPE offered, in conjunction with Fife Regional Council, the first course in Scotland for exercise teachers. From this initial development, course provision has grown, through a variety of pre-graduate modules and courses, alongside in-service course provision and consultancy work. In 1990, Moray House offered the first Certificate in the Teaching of Exercise in Scotland and this proved to be an extremely popular award, with over 200 students successfully achieving the award since it became available. Finally, in 1993, as part of the new postgraduate programme offered by Moray House, a series of postgraduate awards leading to an MSc in Exercise and Health Sciences has been introduced. This award, which is linked to a European inter-university collaboration programme in this area involving twelve European higher education institutions, is proving increasingly popular with a wide range of participants in the fields of exercise, health and fitness.[6]

The Way Ahead

The past decade has seen very substantial development at the Scottish Centre for Physical Education, Movement and Leisure Studies. Its main programme, the single avenue for physical education specialists into Scottish schools, has been developed and strengthened; the undergraduate provision has been extended in the areas of leisure and recreation and in sports science; there has been a substantial expansion of postgraduate opportunities in physical education, dance, outdoor education, and related fields; the centre's commitment to research and development has been maintained; and a number of major centres and activities, important in their own right, have served to create a lively academic environment for students and for staff. The years ahead will require the momentum of development to be maintained. While there will be a modest increase in student numbers, the central lines of development must be to the continued enhancement of undergraduate programmes in association with the physical education profession, and the extension of undergraduate and postgraduate opportunities on the strong base that has been securely laid. In addition, it will be essential for the centre to strengthen its research and development activities to ensure that the vital role it plays in physical education, sport, leisure and recreation will be maintained.

References

1. MacLean, I. C. (1976). *The History of Dunfermline College of Physical Education.* Blackwood & Sons, Edinburgh.
2. *Scottish Tertiary Education Advisory Council Report* (1986). HMSO, Edinburgh.
3. Bayman, D. (1986). 'Undergraduate degrees, postgraduate courses and higher degree provision in physical education and sport'. *Proceedings of VIII Commonwealth and International Conference on Sport, Physical Education, Dance, Recreation, Health.* E & F. N. Spon, 1986.
4. Centre for Leisure Research. (1993). *Graduate Monitoring Study. 1993 Graduates. Final Report.*, pp. 9-14. Moray House Institute.
5. Aitken, M. (1994). 'Cities have to own Sports Colleges' in *The Scotsman*, 28.09.94.
6. Squire, P. (1994). Scottish Journal of Physical Education, Vol. 27, No. 2, pp. 30-32, Exercise and Health Sciences.

4

The Scottish Centre for International Education: From SCEO to SCIE

James W. Morrison

The background

In 1993, with the approval of the Board of Governors, it was decided to change the title of the Scottish Centre for Education Overseas (SCEO) to that of the Scottish Centre for International Education (SCIE). The intention behind this change was to mark a real shift in the focus of our work and in the perceptions – our own and our clients' – of what it is that we have to offer teachers and students from overseas.

The Scottish Centre for Education Overseas was founded to service the British programme of aid to education in the developing world; indeed, the very first courses were commissioned in 1955 by the then Colonial Office. As colonies achieved independence, the need to expand education provision was pressing, especially at the secondary level, which in most cases had been designed to cater for only a small percentage of the population. The first SCEO students, therefore, came from countries which had been British colonies or protectorates. However, especially in response to a growing demand throughout the developing world for English language as a means of access to technology and higher education, the British aid programme was extended to countries which had been within other imperial systems – for example, in Francophone and Lusophone Africa – the rationale being that the spread of British educational models and of the English language was in the long-term political and commercial interest of Britain. There was also a demand for training from independent countries, such as Saudi Arabia or Libya, with oil revenues to spend on developing their education systems.

Thus, for about thirty years from the first dedicated 'overseas' programme in 1955, SCEO was able to rely on a steady demand for courses to train teachers and educational administrators from the developing world. The students were nominated by their governments; they were funded by the British government through the aid programme organised by the Overseas Aid Administration (ODA) or its predecessors; and they were largely administered by the British Council. The staff in SCEO nearly all had direct experience of working in education in the developing world, and a familiarity with the classroom conditions and administrative systems within which trainees would work on their return. Indeed, it is true to say that experience of education overseas was the core qualification; experience in British or Scottish schools was less significant.

Courses were of two kinds: those offering an academic or professional qualification, such as the Diploma in Teaching English as a Second or Foreign Language or the Diploma in Educational Administration, to which individuals were nominated; and those, generally shorter than an academic year, which were specifically designed for a number of students from one particular country. In order to encourage the development of staff expertise and the building up of institutional library and materials resources, ODA developed a policy of directing all aid-funded students in education to five institutions known as the Designated Centres; four of these were in England (in the universities of Bristol, Leeds, London and Newcastle); SCEO was the only one in Scotland and the only one not located in a University. Commenting on this policy, the then Director of SCEO Alexander McLellan wrote in 1985: 'There is nothing sempiternal about this arrangement; it has a short life expectancy and as the pattern of demand in the training needs of overseas governments diversifies, so institutions must be prepared to adapt accordingly; if they fail, it is a short step to diminution and barely a slightly longer one to closure. ODA and the Council will match the need to the service and place the students in the institution that can provide it.'

These were prophetic words, coming as they did shortly before ODA announced its intention to discontinue the Designated Centres policy, in response to pressure both from institutions which were outwith the favoured five and from a Government which was embarking on the 'market force' policies that have changed the face of public service in Britain no less in higher education than elsewhere. What was not foreseen was that ODA and the Council might call into question the desirability of placing students in institutions at all and divert their funds to radically different ways of assisting education overseas. The remainder of this chapter is an account of how SCEO sought to 'adapt accordingly' in the face of changes much more profound than were conceived of in 1985, and how the logic of this process of adaptation led to the change of perception reflected in our new title.

Changes in the market

The first major change was not strictly speaking in the market but in the market-place; that is, the change was not in the services on offer or in demand but in the terms of trade. This was the decision in 1984 to charge the 'full economic cost' of tuition to students from overseas, including students from the British Commonwealth. Apart from the immediate damage to Commonwealth relations (exemplified by the Malaysian response, the 'buy British last' policy) this had long-term consequences for teacher-education institutions.

Firstly, to quote Dr Roger Iredale, Chief Education Officer in the ODA, writing in 1992: 'Government policy has ensured that overseas trainees/students have come to be perceived as an important source of income. Increasingly institutions and departments in them have been developing a new generation of special courses designed specifically to cater for the special needs of identifiable groups . . . This has created a climate of competition, in which some resources traditionally viewed as useful to the aid programme have begun to show signs of strain.'

Secondly, in order to guard against fluctuations in income, especially after the discontinuation of the Designated Centres policy, institutions tended to create a separate cadre of staffing for 'overseas' courses, with a higher proportion than in 'mainstream' courses of staff on short-term contracts. In Moray House, for example, the institutional norm for fixed-term contract staffing is specified in the 1994 Strategic Plan as 15%; in SCIE the 1994 actuality is 50%.

Thirdly, even in those courses such as the PG Diploma in ELT and Linguistics and its successor the MA TESOL, which were relevant to home as well as overseas students, the imposition of full-cost fees and non-availability of grants meant that, except for the rare individual lucky enough to secure sponsorship from the British Council or ODA, these courses were largely confined to aid-funded overseas students. In academic year 1991-92, the last year before the steep decline in British aid funding, of 34 students enrolled on the MA TESOL 33 were funded by ODA; in 1994-95, of 15 students, eight were funded by ODA.

All of these factors, then – separate funding, separate staffing, separate curricula – tended to ghetto-ise overseas education, a tendency reinforced by the fact that overseas students, being mainly experienced teachers undergoing in-service upgrading of qualifications, did not have a great deal professionally in common with Scottish pre-service students. The tension between the desire of overseas students to be integrated with home students, and a perceived need from the sponsor's point of view to ensure against 'the risk that much teaching and material may not be directly relevant to the trainee's home situation' (Iredale, 1992) has been addressed through the SCASI initiative (Sub-Committee for Social and Academic Integration) which reported in 1987, and more recently through the introduction to undergraduate courses of Cross College Modules. However, the essentially different professional interests of students on overseas courses militates against substantive academic integration; and recent developments in the pre-service training of Scottish teachers, with the shift in locus from the Institute to the school, will not facilitate achievement of this objective.

As SCEO entered the 1980s there were 10 recurrent courses bearing an academic award. These were in four areas, and students on English Language Teaching courses, at 45 out of 112, represented fewer than half of total enrolment:

ACADEMIC YEAR 1979-80: AWARD-BEARING COURSES
EDUCATIONAL MANAGEMENT AREA (21 STUDENTS)
Postgraduate Diploma in Educational Management and
    Administration
Diploma in Educational Management and Administration

PRIMARY EDUCATION AREA (20 STUDENTS)
Diploma for Primary Headteachers
Diploma for Primary School Inspectors
Diploma for Primary Teacher Trainers

SPECIAL EDUCATION (26 STUDENTS)
Diploma in Special Education: Retarded and Disadvantaged
    Children
Diploma in Special Education: Visually Handicapped Children
Diploma in Special Education: Deaf and Partially Hearing Children
Diploma in the Teaching of Home Economics

ENGLISH LANGUAGE TEACHING AREA
(45 STUDENTS: 40% OF TOTAL)
Postgraduate Course in Linguistics and English Language Teaching
Diploma in the Teaching of English as a Second or Foreign
    Language

At the time of introducing 'full cost' fees and discontinuation of the Designated Centres policy, the course portfolio in SCEO still covered basically the same areas and with much the same courses. However, English Language Teaching had by now become very much the major focus:

ACADEMIC YEAR 1984-85: AWARD-BEARING COURSES
English Language Teaching (130 students: 76% of total)
Educational Management and Administration (21 students: 12%)
Primary education (6 students: 4%)
Special Education (13 students: 8%)

Little else, however, had fundamentally changed: despite the massive rise in fees, ODA continued through the Technical Co-operation programme to fund students in sufficient quantities to sustain courses; the British Council continued to be responsible for placement and support of these students, the bulk of whom still tended to be directed towards the former Designated-Centre institutions that had developed appropriate courses, staff and resources; and the staff-student ratio remained below 12:1. In the following 10 years, however, changes were to take place – in funding, in courses, in institutional management – at a pace and to an extent previously unimagined.

Changes in course provision

The basic objective of any technical co-operation programme is to assist the recipient country towards self-sufficiency. A fundamental concept of aid, therefore, is that the successful provider works himself out of a job. In the period of major decolonisation (roughly from the end of the '50s to the late '60s) British aid to education largely took the form of cadre-substitution; that is, large numbers of British teachers were recruited to work in new secondary schools and training colleges in the developing world. Once these colleges started producing teachers, and the teachers had some experience, the next stage was to bring them to Britain for courses, largely at diploma level, to enable them not only to replace expensive expatriates in the schools, but also to become trainers themselves. Thus it was always to be expected that training in UK at diploma level – cadre-training – was a transitional phase and that as education and higher education systems were developed, lower-level training would be provided in-country and the level of training for which teachers would need to be sent to Britain would rise.

Degree developments: It was in anticipation of this that SCEO developed the Master's degree in TESOL, validated by CNAA, which graduated its first students in 1985, followed in 1986 by the MSc in Educational Management and Administration. Because many teachers in the developing world were non-graduate products of post-secondary (or indeed post-primary) teacher training colleges, and did not have sufficient academic depth for admission to masters' courses, there was also a need to provide in-service Bachelors' degree programmes to improve career opportunities for these teachers, and in 1988 two new bachelors' degrees, also validated by CNAA, were offered: the BEd (In-Service) ELT, a 1-calendar year course for non-graduate teachers of English, and the BEd (Hons) In-Service Overseas, a 2-academic year course for non-graduate teachers in other disciplines. The BEd (Hons) In-Service Overseas was also a response to the fact that, with the decline in nominations and the constantly eroding staff–student ratio, separate courses in management and the various special education needs were no longer viable; it allowed not only economies in teaching 'education' components but also facilitated viable groups for learner interaction.

The Malaysian connection: Also in 1985, a new 4-year pre-service honours degree, the BEd (Hons) TESOL, was validated through CNAA. This was developed specifically for school leavers selected for teacher-training by the Government of Malaysia, as part of a major initiative to raise standards of English, and was preceded by a 2-year Access Course at Stevenson College in Edinburgh. Though some initial funding assistance was provided by ODA, as a hasty British Government response to Malaysian anger at the imposition of 'full cost' fees on Commonwealth students and the consequences of that anger for British trade, by far the bulk of the programme was – and is, for the programme continues – funded by the Malaysians. (In 1994, when Malaysia again imposed a 'buy British last' policy to signal its displeasure with the British government, the education sector was excluded from the embargo, much to the relief of Moray House, since by that time the Malaysian Government had become a more important client than ODA).

The level of detailed documentation specified in those days for CNAA validation, when CNAA was excessively – some believed obsessively – concerned with demonstrating that its standards were as rigorous as any university's, meant that the validation of two Master's degrees and three Bachelor's degrees in a period of five years demanded a huge effort on the part of SCEO staff, especially as this development time coincided with the onset of annual deterioration in the staff student ratio. Nonetheless, that this major investment in the future was undertaken and completed on schedule was evidence of the readiness of SCEO to adapt to changing demands – and was fully justified by results in the years to follow. Thus, to look ahead, SCEO entered 1984 with *no* full-time students enrolled on degree courses; SCIE entered 1994 with *all* full-time students enrolled on degree courses.

The transition from diplomas to degrees, so long as these continued to attract the support of the funding agencies, ushered in a period of relative planning and teaching stability, in that prior to this (except for a

2-year programme for Saudi trainee teachers of English) all SCEO award-bearing courses had been for one academic or calendar year. The BEd (Hons) TESOL in particular, with four planned intakes each spanning four years, allowed us to make forward staffing commitments on a basis of guaranteed income, as did the BEd (Hons) In-Service Overseas whose students, once recruited, were with us for two years. This stability was welcomed not only by staff on fixed-term contracts but by other heads of department whose staff contributed to SCEO courses.

However, within five years, two factors were radically to alter the scene. These were:

- the UN Inter-Agency World Conference on Education for All in Jomtien, Thailand in 1990.
- the commitment in ODA to Projectisation and Privatisation.

The effect of the first was that it 'encouraged quite fundamental rethinking about the existing traditions of aid and the conventional categories under which it is delivered' (King, 1991). In particular it signalled a shift of focus to the basic education cycle which the Report reckoned could 'be financed within current levels of external assistance to education and training *if most or all of these funds were shifted from post-primary levels to basic education*'. (WCEFA 1990). Concurrent with this, a view was gaining ascendancy that short-term sharply-focussed in-country training was both more efficient and more cost-effective than academic training overseas; indeed, there were those who argued that training should not involve removing teachers from the classroom even for in-service training, but should be delivered 'on-service' (Caillods and Postlethwaite, 1989). The second factor was ODA's response to the political and financial agenda forced on it by Government policies; in particular, privatisation of aid delivery through competitive tendering for projects. Crucially for UK training institutions, projectisation and privatisation destroyed the role of the British Council as central co-ordinator of training placements; as a result, courses which needed to recruit from a number of projects to be viable became unsustainable when there was no central co-ordination of placement. Taken with ODA's decision, suddenly announced in 1992, that there would no new ELT Projects and that all such Projects currently located in Francophone Africa were being withdrawn, it was clear that British aid-funded academic courses intended specifically for overseas students had little future. The speed with which the new ODA policy impacted on SCEO can be seen from the figures over:

	91-92	92-93	93-94
ODA/British Council funded students	186	90	40
ODA/British Council percentage of SCEO funding	67	43	29
ODA-funded Consultancy days overseas	118	78	0
British Council-funded Consultancy days overseas	100	125	42
Number of students from Africa (long and short course)	145	142	38

New directions

Apart from the logic of educational aid being aimed at developing eventual self-sufficiency, the evidence increasingly was that SCEO needed to redefine its self-perception from being a centre of expertise *on* education overseas to being a centre which could promote internationally the Institute's resources, services and staff *for* education overseas. The shifts in aid philosophy (away from cadre-training in UK to capacity-building in-country; away from academic long-course to utilitarian short-course: and away from secondary and tertiary sectors towards basic education) meant not only a reduction in the volume of aid-funded training, but a change in the focus of that training. Increasingly, the reason for bringing overseas teachers to UK would be to provide training for which the capacity did not yet exist in the home country (a declining market) or to provide experience of British expertise and practice (in curriculum design, in methodology, in school organisation, in training).

The repositioning strategy for SCIE included innovation not only in courses, but in the nature of relationships with clients, whether sponsors or students. Examples of such innovations included:

Distance Education: In anticipation of the decline in ODA support for the MA TESOL, from 1992 a major investment in staff time went into developing the MA TESOL by Distance Learning, successfully launched in January 1994. The initial enrolment target of 15 students in the first year was overtaken in six months.

Overseas Institutional Link: In 1992, an agreement was reached with the Malaysian Ministry of Education for a Link with the Specialist Teacher Training Institute in Kuala Lumpur in which a pre-service B Ed (Hons) TESOL degree is taught half in Malaysia and half in Moray House, a programme which will continue until 2001, and under which 5 cohorts of 20 young Malaysians will spend two full academic years in Edinburgh.

New clients: In January 1994, an agreement was signed with the Egyptian Ministry of Education under which teachers of English, Maths and Science undertake 14-week courses, half of the time being spent on attachment in secondary schools in Lothian region; in 1994, three such courses were run, for a total of 208 teachers.

Contract Summer schools: The number of contract summer schools for teachers increased each year: 2 in 1991, 4 in 1992, 5 in 1993, 7 in 1994. Significantly, as for the Egyptians, access to school experience was a condition for one such course; arranging this in Northumberland, Scottish schools already being closed for the summer, typified the flexibility of response cultivated in SCIE.

Commercial language teaching: In 1994, funding was allocated to setting up a commercial English teaching programme, with an opening date of summer 1995.

At the same time, new sources of partnership for research and consultancy led to agreement for a joint research project with Universiti Pertanian Malaysia, and British Council project funding for a research link with Bulgaria, and SCIE staff continued to seek opportunities for overseas consultancy. In 1994 for example, in addition to the British Council, sponsors included The Swedish International Development Agency. That is, the Centre has striven to maintain the full range of activities of an academic department – teaching, research, consultancy – while concurrently developing innovative new programmes for new clients, and all this with a staff base reduced from 14 in 1990 to eight in 1994. The reduction in staff numbers inevitably recalls Alex McLellan's 1985 comment: 'institutions must be prepared to adapt accordingly; if they fail, it is a short step to diminution and barely a slightly longer one to closure'. That view, however, seemed to be based on the assumption that overseas students are serviced by an overseas department. However, to quote examples from 1994, the Egyptian teachers of maths and science were not taught by SCIE department staff; nor were the Malaysian Training College lecturers following a tailor-made short course on Mixed Age/Ability Teaching in the Primary School; nor were the Primary Teachers from the Academie de Clermont Ferrand improving their spoken English. All these programmes were, however, recruited and managed by SCIE.

The future

The incorporation of SCIE as a special Group within the Department of Arts and Humanities at the beginning of session 1994-95, while retaining it as a Directorate, is further evidence of the capacity of the institution to adapt to new circumstances. In so doing, it recognised three realities :

- — that the servicing of overseas courses is an institutional and not a departmental responsibility;
- — that there is a need to develop a perception of SCIE as a facilitator of access to the range of institutional expertise and not merely as an enclave of 'overseas' specialists;
- — that there is a need to extinguish within Departments a residual perception that requests to contribute to overseas courses are a distraction from the 'real' work of the Institute, and that such participation is entirely discretionary.

The approval of the title *Scottish Centre for International Education,* therefore, appropriately recognised significant changes in both the educational concept and in the market, and at the same time re-affirmed the Institute's commitment to maintaining its profile in international education, and to continuing to generate substantial revenues from such activity.

References

Caillods, F. and Postlethwaite T. N. (1989).'Teaching/Learning conditions in Developing Countries', *PROSPECT,* Vol. XIX, No. 2.

Iredale, R. (1992). 'A Review of Training: Needs and Criteria', in Iredale, R. and Sparkhall, K. (Eds.), *The Power of Change.* ODA.

King, K. (1991).'Aid and Education for All (EFA)', in King, K. and Singh, J. S. (Eds.), *Quality and Aid.* Commonwealth Secretariat.

McLellan, A. (1985).'Education Overseas' in Kirk, G. (Ed.), *Moray House and Professional Education.* Scottish Academic Press.

WCEFA (1990). *Meeting Basic Learning Needs: A Vision for the Nineties.* Inter-Agency Commission.

5

Community Education

Lyn Tett

Community education is a young profession. It was first given public policy recognition in 1975 following the recommendations of a Government report entitled 'Adult Education, the Challenge of Change' (The Alexander Report) which resulted in the merger of the informal adult education service with the youth and community work service. The result of this merger was a service unique to Scotland which uses local, dialogical and flexible ways of working with young people and adults in their communities.

The Report sought to create the conditions through which adult education could move from being a leisure pursuit of a more affluent minority who had the confidence to return to educational institutions, to becoming a more relevant and locally based enterprise which involved the mass of people who had traditionally not participated in its provision. The challenge was to escape the conventional syllabi of school-based evening classes and create new and dynamic curricula within communities and community centres which, by their very power of appeal and relevance, would stimulate participation. The joining of adult education together with a numerically far stronger Youth and Community Service, rich in buildings and staff, was expected to provide a range of contacts, insight and understanding for the newly appointed adult educators to respond to (see Steward 1990).

The creation of Community Education Services in most Regional Authorities followed Local Government Reform and led to a clear differentiation between leisure and recreation provision, which was the responsibility of the District Authorities, and educational provision which was the responsibility of the Regions. Within this broad educational focus, however, a range of ideologies of community education practice have been identified. Martin (1987) has constructed a typology of these ideologies based on the implicit models of society and community which underpin practice. These ideologies are described as the 'universal model', the 'reformist model' and the 'radical model'.

Under the universal model it is assumed that there is a consensus with a basic harmony of interests and so universal non-selective provision is made for all ages and social groups. Under the reformist model it is assumed that there are a plurality of interests with inter-group competition for resources and so selective intervention is made to assist disadvantaged people and deprived areas. Finally, under the radical model it is assumed that interests are in conflict because existing structures create inequality and powerlessness. In this model intervention is based on 'developing with local people political education and social action focussed on concrete issues and concerns in the community'.

Investigations of practice (e.g. Kirkwood, 1990; Milburn, 1990) suggest that most workers operate under the 'reformist' model which means that they are most active in communities which suffer from economic and social deprivation. Within these communities workers are responsible for promoting learning activities which can develop people's competence and confidence to become active participants in all aspects of personal and community life and its processes of change.

A Decade of Change and Development

Although community education as such is a young profession, training for one of its components, youth work, has been long established. Moray House was the first Institute in Scotland to provide professional training for youth workers in the form of a one year course which started in 1961. This was later expanded into a two year course and, by the 1970's two and three year courses in youth and community work were available. In the late 1980's all courses in Community Education were reviewed and expertise in informal adult education enhanced to take account of the changes in professional practice. Moray House once again came to the forefront of practice when in 1991 it developed an innovative modular In-Service Master's course in Community Education for experienced practitioners.

Major steps to improve and change the training of professional staff and the part-time and voluntary workers are a reflection of the process of clarifying educational aims and methods in community education.

In relation to training for professional staff the changes that have taken place over the last 10 years are enormous. Since 1985 the pre-service undergraduate qualification has changed from a Diploma in Youth and Community Work to a BA degree in Community Education. The one year Post-Graduate Certificate has been extensively reviewed and now has a two-year part-time route. Three in-service courses have been developed, Master's courses in 'Community Education' and 'Community Development and Health' and a 'conversion course' to enable holders of the Diploma to upgrade their qualification to a Degree. There has also been extensive involvement in In-Service work including National Development work in Fieldwork Supervision and Performance Indicators.

Training for the part-time and voluntary workers who play such an important part in community education was established nationally in 1992 but Moray House was involved in this provision from the 1970's through SESTA. In response to the new national scheme ACT (A Consortium of Training for Community Education) was established. This provides a framework for the development of a progressive system of training suitable for part-time and voluntary workers within the field of community education within the geographical boundaries of Borders, Lothian and Dumfries and Galloway Regional Councils. This initiative built on the work already established through SESTA.

Staff have also experienced a decade of change. Of the present staff only two were here in 1985 and five have been appointed during the last three years. This latter group of staff includes the first ever Director of Community Education.

What has caused all this change? One factor has been the changes in the endorsement of professional training for community education. In 1989 a body was set up by the Scottish Community Education Council, with the agreement of the Scottish Office, to endorse pre-service qualifications in Community Education. Such qualifications were to be modular, competency-based, and of Degree standard. The guidelines produced by the committee, which is called CeVe, required all the courses to be radically revised within a framework which defined Community Education as aiming to:–

- establish effective working relationships with local communities and interest groups, and with other agencies, and to analyse educational needs;
- create, or help others to create, learning opportunities which will meet identified needs;
- ensure that participants become increasingly confident and skilled so that they take responsibility for their own learning and for dealing with other issues of importance to them;
- organise and manage the resources which make possible the delivery of learning opportunities which meet the learners' needs;

- adapt community education to suit the wide variety of contexts which communities across the country are bound to present;
- evaluate practice.

In responding to this competency framework community education staff at Moray House have seen this as a minimal educational objective, not as the purpose of the educational process, whose function is to apply reasoned critique, exposing and clarifying the contradictions which flow from any approach.

The wider intellectual environment which emerges from this broad educational rationale enables students to critically engage with the competences, focusing on the connections (and making explicit the contradictions) between a range of approaches. This has meant providing a structure which helps students to utilise their previous experience, and, where appropriate, make it the starting point for discussion, analysis and development.

Another factor has been the change in the focus of the work of professional community education staff. Within the Local Authority Service the 1980's saw an increasing commitment to generic community education with professional staff as organisers of programmes which were largely delivered by part-time and voluntary staff. In contrast, the voluntary sector employed specialist staff – youth workers, adult educators or community workers who were much more involved in face-to-face work. The 1990's have seen a clearer focus on the community education worker's role as one of informal educator in the community. This means that provision will vary from area to area since a key method of community education is that workers engage in dialogue with local communities regarding the issues identified as important to them. It also means a greater clarity about the purpose and context of intervention with a clear focus on informal educational processes leading to change and development and the growing autonomy of individuals and groups.

In practice, of course, how community educators operate will depend on the constraints of their particular situations, both in terms of the interests of their employers and in terms of the interests of the communities in which they work. The wider political and economic agendas also play a significant role. As Mayo (1994:71) points out there are right-wing versions of community enabling, for example, geared towards the promotion of self-help, to rolling back the State, to reducing service provision, just as there are radical versions of community enabling, with more focus on democratic participation and community empowerment for social transformation. The range of knowledge, skills and understanding that community educators need to practise effectively is therefore very diverse and will always be subject to a critical debate.

Developing Critically Reflective Practitioners

Community Education is not then solely about the delivery of a set of services but rather is a mechanism whereby people are able to reflect on their experience and plan for future action through developing a critical awareness of the issues facing them.

In Moray House we have tried to help this process through both our in-service and pre-service courses by focusing on the development of critically reflective practitioners. The framework within which this takes place is one which sees the student/teacher relationship as fundamentally democratic through dialogical learning. Paulo Freire (1973) argued that for knowledge to be liberating there must be a sense of a common educational purpose between student and teacher and this is the philosophy which underpins our practice.

We also put a great deal of emphasis on theorising practice. The relationship between theory and practice has traditionally been seen as essentially dualistic. Professional practice has been seen as the application of theoretical knowledge to concrete problems. Practice, in itself, is seen, however, as atheoretical in that it neither contains nor generates theory. This way of thinking about professional practice has been described by Schon (1983) as the Technical-Rationality model which sees professional knowledge as a hierarchy in which general principles occupy the highest level and concrete problem-solving the lowest.

This model may be appropriate where professionals apply very general principles to standardised problems but it is not appropriate to the complex, unstable, unique and value-conflict laden world of the community educator. In these situations, problems have to be constructed out of uncertain and confusing situations where the key task is what Schon calls *problem-setting* which is the dynamic process by which the decisions to be made, the ends to be achieved and the means of achieving these ends are determined.

Moreover, reflecting on thought and action is not an individualistic issue because we practise as members of communities whose values, beliefs and norms about the means and ends of practice arise out of particular historical and cultural traditions and are reflected in our daily work. It also means that if we assume that the application of theory is the only certainty of rigour in practice then the achievement of rigour will be purchased at the expense of relevance. This is because where practice situations are uncertain, where ends are not given, then the selection of means cannot be based on the technical application of technically derived principles.

It follows, therefore, that although it is impossible to conceive of practice without theory, the latter may be limited in terms of its articulation, coherence, and consistency. If practitioners 'are to explore their experiences in order to lead to new understanding and appreciation' (Boud *et al*, 1985, p3) of their views about the world, then they need to become aware of what the prevailing norms and 'common-sense' views are that are implicit in their practice.

All participants in community education courses are practitioners since entrants to pre-service courses must demonstrate that they have appropriate experience of at least one of the three main strands of community education. It is therefore particularly important that all students are aware of their 'common sense' assumptions and are able to engage in dialogical reflection on thought and action. This leads to *praxis* because, as Martin (1987: 26) points out, it provides a structure of ideas within which to move from action to reflection and back.

Both pre-service and in-service students will experience tensions and dichotomies within their work if they reflect on their actions because they practice in a world characterised by ideological conflicts, incomplete knowledge, scarce resources, power struggles and infinitely variable human situations. This means that their thinking needs to go beyond the explanation and clarification of assumptions and predispositions, with difficulties addressed by developing inter-subject consensus regarding 'good' practice. Instead we aim to help students become active, informed critics of their own experiences and situations, rather than merely passive respondents to the situations in which they find themselves.

This also means, as Giroux (1992) argues, that:

> *The practice of social criticism becomes inseparable from the act of self-criticism; one cannot take place without the other* (p 79).

Links with the Professions in the Field

Moray House has always ensured that its courses are responsive to the needs of the profession through a variety of formal and informal means. Formally it has a committee called SPICE, chaired by the Principal, which comprises senior professionals from the Community Education Service in Scotland and the voluntary sector which considers any developments in respect of community education. All courses have representation from the profession on their course committees and staff are represented on a number of national and regional bodies in the community education field. Informal contacts between the Institute and the field are also extensive and vital if we are to provide the best possible courses and research.

A particularly interesting development over the last four years has been CONCEPT. This is a Journal of community education practice theory which has an editorial board drawn from all the Institutes providing community education training and community education practitioners from both the statutory and voluntary sectors throughout Scotland. This journal is edited by Moray House staff.

Research and Development

Community education staff at Moray House also make a major contribution to professional development through their research activities. These include empirical research into: the links between community education and further education; how youth work is evaluated; and men's lack of participation in adult education. The findings of this research are disseminated in ways which can be used to bring about change in provision. Other research has been more action-orientated and collaborative involving partnerships between the staff and the field. This is perhaps the most productive of our activities in that it again contributes to our key tasks of developing critically reflective practitioners and ensuring that we are fully aware of the issues and concerns facing practitioners. Work here includes developing anti-sexist/anti-racist work; environmental education; and working with men.

The Journal CONCEPT is an excellent example of the way in which practitioners and staff can work together to theorise practice and write about it in a way that is accessible and stimulating. In particular, it provides a means of encouraging practitioners to critically reflect on their own experience and make a contribution to the creation of a critical culture, where workers can engage with each other and their experiences.

Students too contribute to research and development activities, particularly through their dissertations. Final year pre-service students and all in-service students are engaged in this type of research which makes a contribution to the development of the profession as well as their own professional development.

Continuity and Change

Our work in community education provides continuity, as we look back to the beginnings of our professional training in 1961, and change, when we look to new developments such as the MSc in Community

Development and Health. Our work is both reactive, in responding to the demands of the profession, and pro-active, in identifying new areas and the way forward in dealing with them. The fact that community development has been identified as an appropriate and effective method of tackling problems in the community within a range of issues including health has been instrumental, for example, in guiding this most recent course development.

The community development approach underpins all our work but we are taking a particular interest in health because of the steady increase in the number of projects in community development and health. The training and educational background of practitioners working in the community health field varies enormously. It includes those from teaching, community work, adult education, nursing, social work and health education and those with no formal training. Bringing together a group of people from such diverse backgrounds has enabled us to utilise this range of perspectives as a key learning resource.

The focus changes but the continuity lies in groups of students interacting with each other, engaging with the context and purpose of their practice, attending to their lived experiences, being aware of their 'common sense' assumptions and therefore becoming critically reflective practitioners.

As Collins (1991) points out we should use theory to put ourselves into practice:–

> Though an understanding of theoretical constructions is important to any serious vocational endeavour, it is more efficacious to think in terms of engaging thoughtfully with theory and, then, putting ourselves into practice, rather than putting theory into practice. In other words, serious engagement with theoretical models improves our potential as reflective practitioners, which in turn manifests itself in actual performance (p47).

References

Boud, D. J., Keogh, R. and Walker, D. (Eds.) (1985). *Reflection: Turning Experience into Learning*, London: Kogan Page.

Collins, M. (1991). *Adult Education as Vocation: A Critical Role for the Adult Educator*, London: Routledge.

Friere, P. (1973). *Education for Critical Consciousness*, New York: Seabury.

Giroux, H. (1992). *Border Crossings*, London: Routledge.

Kirkwood, K. (1990). *Vulgar Eloquence: Essays in Education, Community and Politics* Edinburgh: Polygon.

Martin, I. (1987). 'Community Education: Towards a Theoretical Analysis' in Allen *et al* (Ed.) *Community Education: An Agenda for Educational Reform*, Milton Keynes: Open University Press.

Mayo, M. (1994). 'Community Work' in Hanvey, C. and Philpot, T, (Eds.) *Practising Social Work*, London: Routledge.

Milburn, T. (1990). 'The Community Education Service and its Role in Developing Learning Opportunities for Adults' in Corner, T. (Ed.) *Learning Opportunities for Adults*, London: Routledge.

Schon, D. A. (1983). *The Reflective Practitioner: How Professionals Think in Action*, London: Temple Smith.

Scottish Education *Adult Education: The Challenge of Change*, Edinburgh: Department (1975), HMSO.

Steward, T. (1990). 'The Development of Community Education in Scotland Since the Publication of the Alexander Report' in Corner, T. (Ed.) *Learning Opportunities for Adults*, London: Routledge.

6

Education and Training
for Social Work

Ian Mallinson

Introduction

In 1985, social work education and social work practice in Scotland had
experienced a period of over 10 years of stability. The major changes,
brought about by the 1968 Social Work (Scotland) Act, resulting in new
unified Social Work Departments, were based on a generic view of
practice. International perspectives on social work, for example those
developed by Pincus and Minahan (1973), Goldstein (1973), and Bartlett
(1970), defended this generic approach. The structural changes in practice
and in education were derivative of these professional approaches from
the USA.

New generic awards in the UK were established in the early 1970s
by the validating body, the Central Council for Education and Training
in Social Work (CCETSW). CCETSW was founded in 1971, replacing
a plethora of different bodies, each responsible for particular areas of
practice. Specialist awards were phased out. A rudimentary framework
for common standards and requirements was formulated. A common
base of social work education gained ground, focusing particularly upon
family provision, following practice initiatives suggested by The Seebohm
Report, (HMSO, 1968). According to Burrows and Loader (1994), British
social work practice of this period represented the high watermark of
the welfare state and collectivist social policy.

Issues in professional education for social work that were being
debated in 1985 had in common with other areas of British public life
begun to be influenced by economic priorities. Structural cracks in the
nature of the large public welfare monopolies were beginning to be
apparent across all of Europe (Lorenz, 1994). The departments concerned
represented in the UK the market for the output of courses. Political

and economic initiatives now being actively pursued in welfare provision have encouraged a general trend to fragmentation reflecting changing market ideologies within the public sector (Titterton, 1994). The political doctrine of Thatcherism and privatisation has become a world wide phenomena in which the UK took the lead.

A general lack of clarity in the social work role and public debates concerning the legitimacy of social policy implemented by social workers, began to force a grass-roots examination of outcomes in practice assessment. The profession began to examine the nature of work-based requirements and their relationship to academic study.

Two Types of Professional Training

Ten years ago, Moray House already accommodated the largest social work course leading to the Certificate of Qualification in Social Work (CQSW) in Scotland. This had built upon more than twenty years of experience in professional social work education. Expansion in course provision had been a direct response to the growth in numbers of social work staff employed in Scottish authorities. For example, a 21% increase in staff is said to have occurred in regional council social work departments during this period (Morris, 1986.) Growth, stability and a sense of security and purpose were common throughout social work education and social work practice in Scotland at this time.

The CQSW was a three-year full-time course of which the first year at Moray House was a foundation programme shared with Community Education. Many courses elsewhere also had a non-graduate entry but were of two years' duration. The extra year enabled an additional award of a Diploma through The Council for National Academic Awards (CNAA). Access by many students who did not hold formal academic qualifications was part of the philosophy of provision. Academic scrutiny by CNAA as well as professional scrutiny by CCETSW of the quality and level of achievement gave a firm focus to the curriculum and fostered high standards in practice.

Complementary to CQSW was the CCETSW Certificate in Social Service (CSS). This professional course applied to areas of work allied to social work such as residential, day and domiciliary care. CSS was an in-service programme involving projects and other assessment work undertaken within the student's normal job. Moray House's commitment to a scheme involving employers in Lothian, Borders, Central and Fife regions was to provide a focused programme for final studies within the local area. The 'Special Options' involved choices in areas of work with children, adolescents, adults and older people.

Nationally it may be argued that CSS, with its direct focus upon the nature of the student's particular job and its direct learning requirements, was formulated as a reaction to perceived academic isolationism and professional power bases. Certainly, it sought to address a lack of training and perceived poor practice quality in much of the residential and allied sectors of practice (Barr, 1987). Intense national rivalry ensued between CQSW courses, which claimed academic credibility and professionalism, and CSS courses, which claimed relevance and practical competence in social work roles.

The principle of partnership involved in providing CSS was to become highly significant in subsequent developments that moved towards a new generation of qualifying training. CSS schemes, with their clear focus upon learning outcomes related to job requirements, began to establish a reputation amongst employers for achieving improvements in practice and establishing high quality services. As the new economic and political climate developed towards the end of the 1980s, CSS gained in ascendancy over CQSW, although the cost of provision created difficulties. The direct influence of employers in the nature of training outcomes and their clear definition became the political issue within training in the profession. Holders of the CSS award began to exert their expertise and influence on practice despite the initial scepticism of major professional bodies. Similar debates concerning relevance and the confirmation of competence also affected other professional groups during this period.

The first shots in a national debate concerning the relationship between CSS and CQSW were fired in a review of provision conducted by CCETSW in 1982. Serious inadequacies were expressed regarding the ability of existing courses to meet the large increase in social workers' responsibilities. These responsibilities had been established through legislative change introduced since the foundations of training provision had been laid down earlier in the 1970s.

The need for change had been fed by the continual structural shifts in UK social policy (Burrows and Loader, 1994) and by disquiet in the media. Tensions in the social work role concerning the appropriate degree of social control, and when it is appropriate to leave well alone, fed a view promoted by the media of a growing scandal concerning the general competence of social workers. The lack of clarity in social work and its high public profile have possibly affected debates concerning competence and role more than in other professional groups.

The issues in the national debate concerned the extent of training required, the involvement of employers, and the minimising of professional power-bases in order to avoid over-theoretical approaches to practice.

A Single Qualifying Award

The combination of a desire for three year training as decided by CCETSW council in September 1985 and a previous move to a single qualifying award agreed by CCETSW council in July 1984, resulted in the two awards, CQSW and CSS, being regarded as equal. CSS became a social work qualification in its own right. This decision was influenced by a strong management lobby, which welcomed the ability to have a controlling interest in course content, and the continuing failure of professional bodies and practitioners to define what differentiated social work from other forms of intervention.

The problem of cramming a quart into the pint pot of national CQSW training in two years had long been recognised. The Moray House three-year course was unique in the UK. The House of Commons Select Committee in 1983/4 called for an extension of all training to three years. CCETSW was determined to move forward within a variety of full-time and employment-based routes. Collaborative programmes that drew heavily upon CSS were envisaged, with a delicate balance between generic approaches and areas of special emphasis.

In putting its case to the Government for funding, CCETSW said bluntly that social work training had failed to keep pace with demands created by massive change in the previous two decades. Sixty-two new Acts of Parliament with significance for the UK social work task since 1972 were quoted. (CCETSW, 1987). The Government, in the absence of political will, turned down the proposals for a three-year programme on cost grounds. Social work in the UK, it may be argued, appeared alien to the Government's ideal of a low intervention market economy.

CCETSW then framed a new two-year qualification with common standards that was based upon partnership with employers. The regulations for the 'Diploma in Social Work' (DipSW) were contained in the now famous 'Paper 30' (CCETSW 1989), which sought to define a national curriculum of outcomes for social work programmes, based upon practice competency and employer/academic collaboration.

There were considerable tensions and contradictions in the DipSW curriculum, resulting largely from the fact that a quart still had to be put into a pint pot. At Moray House a three year programme at degree level was to be provided. The DipSW requirements were to be fulfilled in two years as elsewhere, but a third year bringing the qualification up to degree standard was instituted. The Moray House DipSW/BA was validated by CCETSW in July 1989.

Areas such as basic management, a greater opportunity for specialism and for evaluative approaches to the social work task formed a major part of the additional third year curriculum. The facility for the third year BA to be taken as an additional qualification on top of professional training (involving candidates holding CQSW or CSS as well as DipSW) rendered this an innovatory scheme. Elsewhere in Scotland the DipSW is taken as a two-year programme also leading to DipHE or in some cases to a master's degree, where candidates have a relevant first degree on entry. Degree programmes lasting three or four years do exist elsewhere in Scotland, but these do not have the facility of exit after two years simply with the DipSW.

Nationally, there remains a basic problem for reduced two-year DipSW programmes. Despite being based upon competency to practise, the DipSW cannot produce workers who are fully competent in all aspects of the social work task. CCETSW has endeavoured to address this issue by instituting additional in-service programmes which give post-qualifying status in specific areas. Some of these are formalised in legislation, such as the requirements for training mental health officers under the Mental Health Act (Scotland) 1984. Most of this provision is agency-based but validated by CCETSW.

The DipSW is said to combine the best of the academic approaches of CQSW with the partnership and collaborative structures of CSS. The Lothian and Borders Training Consortium, consisting of representatives of employers/practice agencies and academic institutions manages on a collaborative basis aspects of DipSW provision, including practice placements, over a wide geographical area. Moray House is an equal partner in these arrangements.

The training consortium is an intermediate body between Moray House and CCETSW. It is influential in establishing quality and standardisation of output and in establishing links between programmes. The consortium is the keystone in the vital bridge of arrangements between the worlds of academic teaching and practice realities. Its committees provide a forum for debate in a world of social work practice that now has an inherent instability.

Developments in Social Policy and Practice

The last ten years have seen considerable change in social work practice and training. New legislation and systems have modified the social work role in agencies beyond recognition.

The framework for the social work task that was gaining currency in 1984 was a response to the Barclay Report (NISW, 1982). The idea here of community based social work, 'based upon developing close working partnerships with citizens, focussing more closely upon the community and its strengths . . . taking full account of informal care, and (mobilising) . . . voluntary and statutory provision in this respect . . .' (NISW, 1982, p 198) took some time to gain a foothold in agencies. Notions of consumerism, partnerships, and localised agendas have now begun to make considerable headway in practice. These developments also appear common to other professional groups. Moray House responded to debates on Barclay by instituting teaching in community social work on the then existing Certificate/Diploma course for qualifying social workers.

In 1989 the Government produced the 'white paper' on policy for Community Care. (HMSO, 1989). The proposals were founded further upon the tide of consumerism and an ideologically perceived need for efficiency in the provision of social work. The new system, enshrined in The National Health Service and Community Care Act 1990, sought gradually to establish market based social care and social work assessment targeting needs . Regional councils have now begun to split services on the basis of a purchaser role in area teams with social workers or their team leaders holding devolved budgets, and provider services, increasingly from the independent sector, meeting defined needs. Individual social workers have become responsible for putting together 'packages of care' to meet specified needs of the 'service user' within specified cost limits.

These moves have heralded for social work a return towards specialist roles within the generic departments and are part of an overall process of fragmentation of local government services. Fragmentation in the 1990s may be suggested as a common theme in much of the work of agencies within the public sector throughout the European Union (Lorenz, 1994). The break up of large monolithic welfare bureaucracies is now common. This process is set to continue in local government in Scotland as a whole, as small unitary authorities are formed which will be largely purchaser rather than provider bodies.

The DipSW curriculum was formulated nationally throughout the UK in 1989 and pre-dated the community care proposals. A CCETSW paper published in 1991 (CCETSW, 1991b) highlighted deficiencies in the national framework. At the time of writing the regulations for DipSW are being rewritten to take account of the changed nature of social work provision and in order to further standardise the curriculum utilising nationally defined schedules of requirements for competency.

Moray House had instituted modules on community care within its DipSW/BA programme in social work in advance of the changes in national and local requirements. This far-sighted move has created firm foundations for the DipSW programme to move firmly through the new developing practice scene of the late 1990s.

Other areas of social work practice have also been subject to change. The most notable area undergoing revision has been that of child care law. Following the implementation of the 1989 Children Act in England and Wales a review was undertaken of Child Care Law in Scotland (Scottish Office, Social Work Services Group, 1993). Whilst the main changes are at the time of writing still under debate, philosophies of practice now begin to reflect principles of partnership in decision-making between workers, children and families. Teaching on the DipSW/BA has reflected such principles of partnership since its instigation and practice initiatives like these have integrated well into its philosophy.

Practice Teaching

As part of a general shift towards competency-based assessment, CCETSW upgraded requirements for on the job/full time placement teaching. At the time of writing no firm date has been set by which both agencies and individual practice teachers will have to have undergone the process of 'accreditation' – that is, trained, approved and registered for placement teaching. In the Lothian and Borders regions most practice teachers participate in accreditation training whilst undertaking work with students. Partly as a result of these requirements and also other priorities emerging in social work departments at a time of rapid change, a national shortfall in DipSW placements has been experienced. The report into child abuse in Orkney (Clyde, 1992) stated that there was an 18% shortfall of DipSW placements in Scotland as a whole. Student intakes at Moray House were reduced in order to manage these issues locally.

Levels of Training for a Competent Workforce

The policy initiatives of CCETSW in formulating the DipSW were founded within a continuum of training awards:

- vocational (or pre- professional);
- professional (for social work – the DipSW); and
- post qualifying/advanced.

This move reflects the establishment of a common national framework for vocational education based upon analysis of job requirements. The committee headed by Charles DeVille was charged with ending the chaos for employers of thousands of different qualifications across all vocational areas. Many of these qualifications did not relate directly to work requirements. The report (MSC/DES, 1986) was influential in setting up a series of national bodies in England and Wales with oversight of each occupational area. In Scotland these powers are vested in one body: the Scottish Vocational Education Council (SCOTVEC).

Several levels of vocational training are now validated jointly by CCETSW and SCOTVEC. Level three of these is combined in Scotland with a Higher National Certificate (HNC). The SCOTVEC courses are competency-based, in the sense that functional analysis of job requirements provides the basis of the curriculum and outcome statements for assessment in the work place or on placement. Considerable debate has taken place regarding the instrumental nature of functional analysis and its ability to provide flexibility and transferability of learning (see for example: Kelly, Payne and Warwick, 1990). It may be argued that the functional mapping of competences undertaken by the various national bodies reflects the erosion of professional power, a diminution of professional knowledge bases and a process of de-skilling, as much as achieving a fully competent workforce and common qualifications.

The HNC at Moray House was instituted in 1992. It seeks to combine competency in practice with an ability to reflect and analyse. It thus is able to function more clearly as access provision for the BA in social work, than similar provision elsewhere in Scotland.

Current modifications to the DipSW requirements and regulations under national UK consideration are utilising the approach of functional analysis of the social work task in order to prescribe a national curriculum. It remains to be seen what the full impact of these proposals will be.

The main formulation of CCETSW's proposals for the continuum emerged in CCETSW Council meeting during the academic year 1989-90. This coincided with the creation at Moray House of the new Department of Social Science and Social Work. A new training framework provided part of the impetus for a realignment of professional areas.

Post-Graduate Provision

The changed requirements of new community care systems created pressure upon middle and senior managers. The need for strategic planning in order to manage more fragmented services efficiently and effectively is one of the major issues here. Utilising the Moray House modular masters scheme a new integrated postgraduate certificate, diploma/master of science award was created to meet these advanced level needs. The Masters degree started in 1994. It represents the summit of a ladder of opportunities that focus upon professional development needs within the context of immediate requirements in work settings.

The experience of social work staff in the arena of community care planning and community care management has been a major thread in matching experience and needs. The philosophy of the MSc is that whilst there are generic management needs that apply across all forms of management (business and public sector/ different professional areas) some significant specific fields of study are appropriate to the social services arena. This differentiates the degree from other qualifications given elsewhere, such as Masters of Business Administration.

Conclusions

Ten years of social change have forced considerable revisions in the nature of social work practice. Nationally, educational responses to this have generally been reactive rather than proactive. The most significant feature of the decade has been the production of a competency-based curriculum located in a framework of levels relating to requirements in the workplace. The tensions between instrumental approaches to learning for a prescribed view of the social work task and wider analytic learning is still unresolved in continuing national debates.

Social work education at Moray House has created workable solutions within these tensions. The pace of change is continuing and the next decade will almost certainly result in many further modifications to curriculum and methodology on all Moray House programmes. The capacity to work with new requirements and to take a proactive approach to development have characterised the activities of social work staff over the last ten years and will certainly continue to provide the basis for provision in the years ahead.

References

Barr, H. (1987). *Perspectives on Training For Residential Work*, Central Council for Education and Training in Social Work, London.

Bartlett, H. M. (1970). *The Common Base of Social Work Practice,* National Association of Social Workers, New York.

Burrows, R. and Loader, B., (Eds.) (1994). *Towards a Post-Fordist Welfare State?* Routledge, London.

CCETSW (1987). *The Qualifying Diploma in Social Work, A Policy Statement,* Paper 20.8. Central Council for Education and Training in Social Work, London.

CCETSW (1989). *DipSW Rules and Requirements for the Diploma in Social Work,* Paper 30. Central Council for Education and Training in Social Work, London.

CCETSW (1990). *The Requirements for Post Qualifying Education and Training in the Personal Social Services,* Paper 31. Central Council for Education and Training in Social Work, London.

CCETSW (1991a). *DipSW Rules and Requirements for the Diploma in Social Work.* Paper 30. Second Edition, Central Council for Education and Training in Social Work, London.

CCETSW (1991b). *Assessment Care Management and Inspection in Community Care, Towards a Practice Curriculum*, Improving Social Work Education and Training, Five. Central Council for Education and Training in Social Work, London.

Clyde, Lord (1992). *The Report of The Inquiry into The Removal of Children from Orkney in February, 1991*, HMSO, Edinburgh.

Goldstein, H. (1973). *Social Work Practice a Unitary Approach*, University of South Carolina Press, Colombia.

Griffiths, Sir Roy (1988). *Community Care: Agenda for Action: A report to the Secretary of State for Social Services*, Her Majesty's Stationery Office, London.

HMSO (1968). *Report of The Committee on Local Authority and Allied Personal Social Services*, Her Majesty's Stationery Office, London.

HMSO (1989). *Caring for People, Community Care in The Next Decade and Beyond*, Her Majesty's Stationery Office, London.

Kelly, D., Payne, C. and Warwick, J. (1990). *Making Vocational Qualifications Work for Social Care*, National Institute for Social Work/Social Care Association, London.

Lorenz, W. (1994). *Social Work in a Changing Europe*, Routledge, London.

MSC/DES (1986). *Review of Vocational Qualifications in England and Wales, Manpower Services Commission*, Department of Education and Science, London.

Morris, P. (1986). 'The Growth Industry of The 1980s in Scotland', *Community Care*, 23-10-86.

NISW (1982). *Social Workers Their Role and Tasks*. The Barclay Report, National Institute for Social Work, London.

Pincus, A. and Minahan, A. (1973). *Social Work Practice: Model and Method*, Peacock, Itaska.

Titterton, M., (Ed.) (1994). *Caring for People in The Community: The New Welfare*, Jessica Kingsley, London.

7

The Modular Master's Scheme

John Landon

Background

Ten years ago, to a member of staff at Moray House in-service training meant an informal contact from an educational authority adviser or a regional training officer, followed by one or more training sessions at a teachers' centre or other agency. There was very little accountability, scant involvement in decision-making about training by the trainees themselves, a poor sense of the continuity of training and development and almost no competition for the training market. From today's standpoint, this scene is barely recognisable.

In 1984, two reports which addressed some of these shortcomings were submitted to the Secretary of State by the National Committee for the In-service Training of Teachers (NCITT). These two reports, *Arrangements for the Staff Development of Teachers* and *The Development of the Three Tier Structure of Award-Bearing Courses*, presented a new view of staff development as a planned and co-ordinated process, supported by explicit institutional policies, consisting of activities matched to institutional and individual needs, and offering the opportunity for continuous professional enhancement.

During this period, the government gave direct funding to training institutions to cover the salaries of staff engaged in in-service activities. At Moray House this allowance amounted to nearly 25 per cent of the College's total staffing entitlement in the 1983/84 session. However, despite the rhetoric of planning, co-ordination, partnership and continuity, staff development programmes continued to be planned and implemented according to a 'top-down' model. Course members were perceived as being in receipt of training delivered paternalistically by the training institution, sometimes circumscribed by guidelines issued by national bodies set up to co-ordinate training. With the adoption of the three-tier course structure, introduced by NCITT, such training increasingly led to awards at Certificate level (after one term of full-time study, or part-time equivalent), Diploma level (the Diploma in Professional Studies in Education, DPSE, awarded after four terms of full-time study) or Master's level. Moray House began to offer a number of Certificate and DPSE level courses, validated by the Council for National Academic Awards (CNAA). These tended to be upgrading courses for teachers, which concentrated on the improvement of professional practice in a fairly restricted technical sense.

Following a change of government policy, direct funding to training institutions to cover the salaries of staff engaged in in-service activities was phased out between 1989 and 1991, and was replaced by grants made directly to education authorities and other public sector providers. The emphasis changed from supply to demand. The training providers were held more accountable to the funding agencies, who increasingly required value for money, partnership in the training process and evidence of quality. In order to maintain the staffing levels previously supported from central funding, the colleges responded by seeking contracts for consultancy work and by increasing the extent and range of award-bearing courses. They also started to compete with each other for the market, by extending their in-service activities beyond their previous geographical boundaries. During this period, the training institutions began to see the demand for training diminishing, as authorities and agencies looked elsewhere for training, or used their budgets to provide training themselves. The training provided at local level was non-award bearing and was concerned with the development of practical or managerial skills, related to the implementation of government policy. The training institutions, facing growing competition and aspiring to university status with the breakdown of the binary division of higher education, needed to rethink the nature of the staff development opportunities which they were providing.

There is no doubt that in-service training at Moray House underwent an identity crisis at this point. There was reluctance to acknowledge the demise of the essentially practical award-bearing courses leading to the Certificate or DPSE. The CNAA was shortly to be disbanded as the non-university sector validating body. Moray House was seeking closer links with Heriot-Watt University, which would become the new validating body. It was recognised also that the pattern of funding of training was likely to change again with a shift of resources for staff development from regional to local school or agency level. At this stage, discussions began at Moray House about a new award-bearing structure with a redefinition of rationale and aims. Two Master's level awards were already offered by the Scottish Centre for Education Overseas in Teaching English to Speakers of Other Languages (TESOL) and Educational

Management and Administration (Overseas) and the MA Leisure Policy was available through the Scottish Centre for Physical Education, Movement and Leisure Studies (SCOPEMALS). To these were added Master's level programmes in Community Education, Cultural Services Management, Sports Coaching and in the field of Teacher Education, in Special Educational Needs, and Computers and Learning. Most of the existing Diploma in Professional Studies in Education (DPSE) programmes were upgraded with the introduction of a requirement for reflection on, and analysis, of practice, in accordance with the findings of current published research and of action research. A framework for standardising and coordinating the development of Master's level programmes was validated in October 1991, and so the Modular Master's Scheme was born.

Rationale of the Scheme

The rationale for the Scheme is concerned with the definition of study at Master's level, and with the relationship of theoretical knowledge to practical application in what the documentation describes as 'a professional Master's degree' (as opposed to the academic theoretically-weighted higher degrees of traditional universities). The framework document begins:

> *The Scheme is intended to assist course members to confront their own professional practice in a spirit of rational critical enquiry.*

Thus, the rationale is seen to be firmly embedded in the notion of the reflective practitioner (Schon 1983) working within a critical enquiry framework which assists in the analysis and understanding of experience in relation to wider professional concerns (Carr and Kemmis 1986). It is argued that:

> *this kind of study provides course members with the confidence to be more proactive, both within their own institutional context and in the wider arena, thereby benefiting their professional work* (Moray House 1991).

The development of such critical proactivity is carried out through the content and the delivery of the programme. Course content provides students with an in-depth understanding of the theoretical and socio-political context in which professional decision-making takes place. It also enhances the meta-professional skills of problem identification and analysis, action research, and monitoring and evaluation and strengthens competences and strategies for managing change. This is applied not only within the course member's professional context, but also to the process of planning the programme of study. Here, course members are supported in analysing their own staff development needs both in the light of their own experience and within the context of changes within their institution or profession, and are provided with a flexible framework for articulating those needs within a programme of study. This process is not intended to be prescriptive, but dialogic, characterised by negotiation between the trainee and the training institution. Thus, critical reflection is both the medium and the message of the Scheme.

One important aspect of negotiation of a training contract (for that is essentially the spirit of the arrangement) between Moray House and the course member is the recognition for credit purposes of recent and appropriate prior learning or experience. This is important for encouraging course members to reflect upon their current level of theoretical understanding and related professional competency. It also facilitates the articulation of work-based professional development programmes or nationally agreed standards of professional competence with the learning outcomes outlined within Moray House programmes. The principles of flexibility and partnership which were so often absent from earlier programmes are therefore enshrined within the Modular Master's scheme.

Structure of the Scheme

Watson (1989) has commented on the Oxford Polytechnic Modular Course in these words:

> The Modular Course is, in this sense at least, a misnomer. The Modular Scheme is fundamentally an organisational device which, while requiring appropriate rigour for the achievement of recognised academic awards, allows for an immense variety of individual pathways to their achievement. There are potentially as many 'Modular Courses' as there are students registered on the Scheme.

Such is the spirit behind the rationale and structure of Moray House's Modular Master's Scheme, but, as in life, so in institutional policies, the spirit is willing but the flesh is weak.

The Scheme framework was essentially a *post hoc* 'modular' rationale for a number of discrete award-bearing courses with 'unitised' structures. In spite of the framework document, modularity continued as a pretence as new unitised pathways were added with regulations which did not allow for the flexibility and choice which the Scheme intended. Modules were seen as 'belonging to' pathways with tight rules regarding progression and selection; they were not conceived as free-standing elements which could be chosen and combined according to the course member's professional development needs. The paternalistic model whereby the course planner decides what content should be studied and in what order has been difficult to break through, and has impeded the coming-of-age of the course member emancipated to make her/his own professional development decisions. This is not to say that a truly flexible modular programme does not present its challenges. The challenges were not addressed because they were not recognised until the validation of the Open Masters in November 1992 and its implementation the following year.

As the Open Master's Regulatory Framework states:

> The Open Master's provides the opportunity for professionals to plan and undertake their own development outside the constraints imposed by a titled pathway. It enables professionals to tailor their own development programme at Master's level to their own needs, aspirations and interests. (Moray House 1992).

The Open Master's redefined the nature of the Modular Master's Scheme by recognising structurally that modules belong to the Scheme as a whole, and that pathways are the combination of modules required within a validation document for the achievement of a titled award. Thus, possible within the Scheme, are the selection, combination and progression of modules according to the course member's own definition of coherence and progression for the Open award, as well as regulations, of more or less prescriptiveness, for the choice and progression of modules leading to specialist titled awards. Currently the Scheme includes modules in the following professional areas, each with their own specialist award: Teacher Education (including Aesthetic Studies, Computers and Learning, Counselling, Dance, Early Education, Educational Management, Guidance, Outdoor Education, Special Educational Needs, Specific Learning Difficulties), Community Education, Social Service Management, Cultural Policy and Management, Coaching Studies, Exercise and Health, Leisure Policy and Practice and Teaching English to Speakers of Other Languages. These may be combined, in part-time or full-time mode, over a period from one to six years, towards a Postgraduate Certificate (4 modules), Postgraduate Diploma (10 modules) or Master's award (10 modules plus an Extended Study), or can be taken on their own as free-standing modules.

Current Issues and Challenges

So far, apart from the difficulties inherent in the evolution from a unitised pathway-based, to an integrated modular structure, the conception of the Modular Master's Scheme has been presented as relatively unproblematic. This belies the considerable amount of discussion currently underway within the Institute, and the wider academic community, about the definition of Master's level work, the preferred structure, balance and progression of a programme leading to a Master's award, and the sometimes uneasy relationship between flexibility and openness on the one hand and academic and professional integrity on the other. There are also questions relating to quality assurance across such a diverse scheme, and the maintenance of standards as the Scheme develops through partnership with other institutions and through a variety of modes of delivery. Finally, there are challenges to the Institute as a whole with regard to its responsiveness to a volatile market, and its strategies for broadening the staff base, and for developing its expertise and resources, to sustain its expanding post-qualifying award-bearing programme.

These challenges cannot be addressed in a leisurely way because the pressures of change and the demands of the market are too great. There must be thorough and wide-ranging discussions, involving professional partners in the public services, colleagues involved in education and training, and those who are charged with the external scrutiny of the Institute's work.

Master's Level Work: Within a very short time, our understanding of educational level, based upon the taken-for-granted assumptions which a closely knit 'knowledge community' can safely assume that it shares, and thus 'take on trust' (Winter 1994), has been challenged by exposure to three novel notions. Firstly, the definition of level understood within one professional area, say teacher education, has somehow to correspond to the definition in another professional area, say cultural policy, in a flexible modular scheme which allows students a choice of modules from across a variety of professional areas. Secondly, the expansion of the 'knowledge community', and thereby the definitions of level within it, is challenged by the possibility of credit being awarded for prior learning or experience in a wide variety of other institutions over much longer periods than the conventional one-year full-time course. Thirdly, definitions based on traditional academic criteria, like criticality, analysis, integration of theory and practice, and research, now have to sit alongside those deriving from the industrial lead bodies, which are based upon understanding of the structure of organisational life and their attendant occupational functions. Here, Master's level is defined as 'competence which involves the application of a significant range of fundamental principles and complex techniques across a wide and often unpredictable variety of contexts. Very substantial personal autonomy and often significant responsibility for the work of others and for the allocation of substantial resources feature strongly, as do personal accountabilities for analysis and diagnosis, design, planning, execution and evaluation'. (NCVQ 1991).

Within Moray House's Modular Master's Scheme, the general criteria for Master's level work which characterise the Scheme as a whole are increasingly required by the demands of professional bodies and employers to sit alongside criteria relating to professional competence in the workplace. This association is sometimes uneasy as it sets a strain upon the relationship between theory and practice in the expectations which students have about the nature of the programme content and delivery and their understanding of the nature of the study which is to be undertaken. It also challenges the competence of lecturing staff who traditionally have felt obliged to keep abreast of the academic literature but who now have to discover new ways of enhancing the practical relevance of the course, by engagement in practice themselves, through partnership in delivery with practitioner-trainers who will serve to contextualise theoretical knowledge (Day and Pennington 1994), or through the development of new patterns of delivery, which utilise student experience, or which are based on learning contracts negotiated between external clients (employers), the students and the training institution (Stephenson and Laycock 1993).

Moray House is facing these challenges in a number of ways. First of all, in recent validation documents and in the practice of grading assignments, a distinction is being made between general learning abilities (Winter 1994) which define the theoretical model on which the Scheme is based and characterise the Scheme as a whole, and the specific learning outcomes and performance criteria of particular modules, which may be related more closely to competency outcomes within professional contexts. Proposals are in hand to appoint an external examiner for the whole Scheme who will keep an overview of the general standards of the Scheme across all modules, whilst other external examiners concentrate on the maintenance of standards within specific professional areas.

There are also interesting innovations designed to break down the barriers between the theory-oriented classroom and practical application in the workplace. Traditionally, evidence of practical application has been drawn from a placement which has been the equivalent of one module of a diploma programme. This is clearly inadequate as a means of assessing the student's ability to relate theory to practice and to demonstrate professional competence. It also fails to exploit the fact that a part-time course member is usually employed within a professional 'laboratory' which provides the perfect context for action research, innovation and evaluation. All of these are skills which will continue to develop within the work context once the programme of study is finished, thus realising some of the long-term goals of continuing education. Some pathways have introduced the requirement to produce a portfolio as part of the ongoing work of the programme. In the portfolio, course members assess strengths and weaknesses on the basis of an appraisal of past and present achievements and the pressures and opportunities of their work setting, and, using this information, produce an individual development plan. This plan they put into operation both within the taught course programme and within their work context, and through the portfolio reflect on their ongoing performance (Harrison 1993). This approach is becoming increasingly common through the Records of Achievement movement in schools and further education (Assiter and Shaw 1993) and within the working requirements of some professions such as nursing (Rolfe and Jasper 1993) and social work (Thomas 1993).

The other area of innovation is partnership with professional bodies involving joint training. By this arrangement the Institute provides the theoretical underpinning which is contextualised through practical training and self- and peer-assessment within the workplace. Currently, discussions are being held with training officers in social work and with the training sections of a number of counselling agencies. There is considerable scope for this kind of cooperation within each of the professional areas served by the Institute. However, at present, within teacher education the linear staff development continuum which begins so promisingly with partnership through the mentorship programme is not sustained by support for partnership in school-based action research projects or in-service accredited programmes as part of an on-going multi-dimensional model of professional development (Day and Pennington 1994). Cooperation towards the establishment of such a scheme has begun with some independent schools in Edinburgh, and through the development of accredited action research modules at Moray House. The devolvement of resources for training to local agencies, like schools, will require the growth of new kinds of collaborative programmes of professional development which are partly or wholly agency-based, in which the employing agency will assume a more powerful role, and which will contribute not only to individual professional development but also to institutional change (Hargreaves 1994).

Reviewing the Scheme's Structure: Over the past five years, the Modular Master's Scheme has grown from approximately 50 modules to 250. The number of awards has developed from eight to 30. The challenge of developing systems and an administrative infrastructure to cope with such a range of choice has allowed little time to reflect upon the appropriateness of the Scheme's structure.

As has been discussed, the Scheme has evolved in a relatively unplanned way. Now the same modules may be combined, according to fairly strict rules of selection and progression, to lead to specialist titled awards, or combined flexibly and cross-professionally, towards an open award. In the former case, it is in the interests of a phased development of theoretical understanding and academic coherence that the rules have been formulated; in the latter case, it is the individual's personal or professional development needs which govern choice, and frequently the availability of modules which dictates progression. Thus, within the same module there can be a student who is nearing the end of a specialist diploma programme and a student who is undertaking a first module in that particular professional area.

It is clear that the market is attracted by flexibility and is deterred by prescriptiveness. However, flexibility of choice which ignores the need for some sense of progression and development of understanding, building specialist applications upon basic principles, creates a strain for both course members and lecturers. Furthermore, a broad array of specialist pathways, each with their own structure and balance of required modules (often perceived as presenting core principles) and electives (specialist applications), can be confusing.

There is already within the Modular Master's Scheme a movement towards generating award-bearing programmes from clusters of modules within specific professional areas. The difference between this approach and the traditional prescriptive and complex pathway model lies in the degree of choice permitted and the simplicity of the course structure. The MEd programme provides a model for this, which could be developed within other professional areas. There are discussions currently underway about a Master's degree in public service management which will allow choice from any of the management modules in the Scheme. A certain percentage will be designated as required at certificate level, and certain others will be required at diploma level. Similar professional groupings, with modules classified in this way could form the basis of other titled awards, for example in sport, leisure, community education, special educational needs and social work. The designation of certain modules as required at certain levels of the Scheme could also serve to introduce a greater sense of progression within the Open Master's award, and help solve the logistical problem, within any Scheme with a high degree of optionality, of module viability.

If progression can be safeguarded through this modification to the Scheme, a sense of coherence can be introduced into the more flexible model by requiring at the outset of any course of study what Winter (1994) calls an 'Integrative Unit', thus 'ensuring that at the centre of the student choice lies the student's conscious sense of relevance and purpose, not merely the contingent system of available learning units'. The Professional Development module, which is at present required for the Open award and within a number of other pathways, could serve this function, through its consideration of the nature of professionalism and professional development and its application of the principles in individual programme planning.

Outreach and Development: The Modular Master's Scheme is administered from the Institute's Professional Development Centre. Here academic and administrative staff cooperate in coordinating modules delivered within the Institute and those taught on an outreach basis, which have been contracted by agencies or local authorities. Staff development at a postgraduate level is an extremely competitive market. The Institute is, therefore, constantly considering ways of extending the marketability of modules within the Scheme. One approach is through staff development partnerships with schools, colleges, agencies and regional authorities. Another is through franchising modules or awards for delivery at another institution. A third approach is to increase the accessibility of modules through the development of open and distance learning opportunities both at home and overseas.

Each of these approaches is already being implemented in an embryonic way. Partnerships with further education institutions are under discussion, and have already begun in the area of management training. In social service management and counselling there are plans to articulate the Institute's modular programme with regional or agency staff development provision leading to postgraduate awards. Such partnerships are useful not only in opening up training opportunities but also in consolidating the applied practice base required for professional development at this level.

One form of partnership is the development of a franchise arrangement between two institutions (Yorke 1993). In this way, the Institute approves another institution or consortium of institutions in Britain or overseas to deliver, as franchisees, an award-bearing course, a module or cluster of modules previously validated by the University. The philosophy behind a franchise agreement is that there remains one course, the difference being in the context of delivery. Thus, the staff of the franchisee institution become full members of the one course team, in terms of participating in course management, course assessment and course development. The advantages for the Institute of franchise partnerships are that they bring Institute staff into close professional contact with colleagues in other institutions, thus establishing a network for mutual development. They also establish the Institute's leadership in professional areas in which its expertise has long been acknowledged. The current challenge to the Institute is to establish effective quality assurance procedures to ensure the maintenance of the standards of franchised courses operating in other institutions.

Finally, following initiatives implemented by the Institute's Scottish Centre for International Education (SCIE) in developing Master's level modules in TESOL in distance learning mode, the Institute is considering the implications of developing further modules for distance learning. This requires considerable investment in staff time to produce modules, and the resources necessary to establish the systems necessary to sustain an enlarged distance learning operation (Morrison 1993). Other approaches to flexible learning will also need to be considered so that students may have access to learning opportunities at their convenience, and so that the Institute can obviate the necessity of requiring a viable class size before a module can run.

Conclusion

The implementation of the Modular Master's Scheme has necessitated considerable structural changes in the Institute. Together with these have come a number of challenges to the traditional role of academic staff. The Scheme, first of all, requires complex data-handling systems to cope with the number of options available to course members. These have to be centralised. They have, therefore, had the effect of reducing the role of academic staff in course management. The degree of flexibility and choice within the Scheme, especially since the introduction of the open award, has shifted the responsibility for programme planning from academic staff to course members, and has, thus, changed the teaching staff's traditional sense of ownership of the programme and their perceived right to impose cohesion and progression on the structure of teaching and learning. In a highly competitive market, there are also unfamiliar pressures upon lecturing staff to develop models which are maximally flexible, so that they can be adjusted to correspond to market requirements. The market has its own agenda, which is frequently expressed not in terms of theoretical concepts but in terms of occupational competences, which are determined by functional analysis rather than by academic considerations.

As the Scheme develops, each of these issues needs to be open to discussion and review. It is important, at a time of rapid change and unprecedented external pressures, that Institute staff, together with partners in professional development, both students and employers, should reflect upon the definition and maintenance of standards and upon ways of forming the most effective partnerships. In short, the principles of reflective practice and critical proactivity which lie at the heart of the Scheme's rationale must also form the basis of the Scheme's development.

References

Assiter, A. and Shaw, E. (Eds.) (1993). *Using Records of Achievement in Higher Education*, Kogan Page, London.

Carr, W. and Kemmis, S. (1986). *Becoming Critical: Knowing Through Action Research*, Deakin University, Open Campus Programme, Geelong, Australia.

Day, C. and Pennington, A. (1994). 'Conceptualising Professional Development Planning: a Multidimensional Model', *International Analysis of Teacher Education, Special Issue of Journal of Education for Teaching*, 19, 4 and 5, pp. 251-260.

Hargreaves, D. (1994). 'The New Professionalism: the Synthesis of Professional and Institutional Development', *Teaching and Teacher Education*, 10, 4, pp. 423-438.

Harrison, R. (1993). 'Using Portfolios for Personal and Career Development' in Assiter, A. and Shaw, E. (Eds.), *Using Records of Achievement in Higher Education*, Kogan Page, London.

Moray House (1991). *Modular Master's Scheme Part II Documentation*, Moray House Institute of Education, Heriot-Watt University, Edinburgh.

Moray House (1992). *Open Master's Regulatory Framework*, Moray House Institute of Education, Heriot-Watt University, Edinburgh.

Morrison, J. (1993). 'The Costs of Distance Education', *Report of Dunford Seminar, Language Issues in Distance Education*, British Council, Manchester.

NCVQ (1991). *Criteria for National Vocational Qualifications*, National Council for Vocational Qualifications, London.

Rolfe, G. and Jasper, M. (1993). 'Some Strategies for Curriculum Development in Nurse Education', *Journal of Further and Higher Education*, 17, 3, pp. 105-111.

Schon, D. A. (1983). *The Reflective Practitioner: How Professionals Think in Action*, Basic Books, New York.

Stephenson, C. and Laycock, M. (Eds.) (1993). *Using Learning Contracts in Higher Education*, Kogan Page, London.

Thomas, D. (1993). *Portfolio Guide: Management Education Scheme by Open Learning*, Open Learning Foundation and Open University, Milton Keynes.

Watson, D. (1989). *Managing the Modular Course, Perspectives from Oxford Polytechnic*. SRHE and Open University Press, Milton Keynes.

Winter, R. (1994). 'The Problem of Education Levels, Part II: A New Framework for Credit Accumulation in Higher Education', *Journal of Further and Higher Education*, 18, 1, pp. 92-106.

Yorke, M. (1993). 'Quality Assurance for Higher Education Franchising', *Higher Education*, 26, pp. 167-182.

8

Teaching and Learning

Brian D. Cosford, Robert W. McNie, Hugh E. Perfect and Donald Skinner

Introduction

Recent research on the nature of learning in higher education, increased accountability to professional and accrediting bodies, and the changing economic realities of higher education during the past decade have led the Institute to reassess its policy on teaching and learning to ensure that its commitment to excellence is realised in a way matched to the rapidly changing context of higher education.

External influences such as the SHEFC Quality Assessment have highlighted the need to focus attention in much more detail on teaching and learning in *higher education* in addition to the Institute's more traditional focus on primary and secondary teaching. Other changes in the nature of higher education, including the introduction of the competency approach in vocational education by the SOED, CCETSW and SCEC, the move towards modularisation, and a policy of increased access to higher education have also helped to focus attention on the quality of teaching and learning and the need for further innovation. The potential of information technology to support the teaching and learning process is increasingly acknowledged and is being tested, for example, by such major initiatives as the Teaching and Learning Technology Programme supported by the higher education funding councils.

A History of Innovation

No institution stands still in its approach to teaching, and changes in the educational climate have led Moray House to question some of its assumptions about the learning needs of students and to reconsider the role of academic staff as higher education teachers. Moray House has played a leading role in most school-based innovations in curriculum development for one and a half centuries (Bain, 1985) and in recent decades this has been achieved by the very intensive involvement of academic staff in national development programmes, consultancy work, staff development and research. Teaching and learning are now high on the agenda of all higher education institutions. The presence of this chapter contrasts with the sister Moray House publication (Kirk, 1985) where consideration of teaching and learning appears only tangentially in relation to other concerns.

Moray House serves a number of professions, including social work, community education, teaching, and leisure and recreation. Hall and Black, in a SCRE seminar (Hall and Black, 1993) on the MacFarlane Report (MacFarlane, 1992) asked 'Do teachers in higher education share the same perceptions of teaching?' This is a question that requires detailed investigation but we suggest that for those working in teacher education, whose role includes the education and training of future generations of teachers, innovation in teaching methods is particularly important. Colleges and faculties of education, we suggest, differ from other higher education institutions, because the primary task of a majority of the academic staff is the dissemination and creation of the theory and the practice of *teaching*.

Conceptions of Teaching Methods in Higher Education

Whilst in recent years the field of higher education has seen a proliferation of projects on 'innovative teaching methods' (Gibbs, 1992), sustained research on key aspects of student learning (Entwistle and Tait, 1990, Entwistle, 1992, Marton, et al 1992) and discussions of the impact of information technology on teaching (Laurillard, 1993), there has been no sustained, critical exploration of current conceptions of the range and variety of teaching methods that effective higher education now demands. Even the MacFarlane report (MacFarlane, 1992) resorts unquestioningly to traditional categories (lectures, tutorials, practicals, etc) in its otherwise forward-looking discussion of teaching and learning issues. The analytic effort has so far focused on conceptions of learning at the expense of conceptions of teaching. Clear thinking in relation to both, however, is required for systematic policy development and to give direction to staff development.

In Moray House a research project initiated in 1993 on the typology of teaching methods in higher education is addressing this issue, exploring the variety of teaching and learning in higher education and considering how far conceptions of the nature and range of teaching methods, which have proved fruitful in other sectors of education, might also prove useful in discussing teaching in higher education (Cosford, McNie and Skinner, 1993).

What possibilities exist for categorising teaching in higher education? At present, discussions tend to focus on 'traditional versus innovative' teaching methods and are essentially concerned with a move away from lectures and didactic teaching towards 'student-centred' methods such as role play, new forms of group interaction and applications of information technology to teaching, thus paralleling in higher education the long-standing controversy in school education between traditionalists and progressives. Unless the discussion develops further, however, the debate may prove equally sterile, although the push for innovative methods has certainly helped to stimulate thinking and experiment. However, to date the host of new approaches have been inadequately conceptualised. Lecturers have no clear basis for making decisions about which methods to use and when. Some deeper conceptual framework for decision-making is clearly required.

The Moray House project on higher education teaching methods is exploring the potential of the theory of 'teaching modes' as a basis for this framework. This theory, first developed at Stirling University under Professor Morrison (Peacock, 1990) for training secondary teachers, was soon taken up by the Committee for Primary Education in 1983 as a framework for thinking about teaching in primary schools (CCC, 1983). A similar analysis informed the 16-18 Action Plan (SED, 1985) and more recently has emerged as the main basis for discussions of teaching methodology in the 5-14 Development Programme. It currently underpins the Moray House staff development initiative on 'The Reflective Practitioner in Higher Education.' The basic idea is that at any level of education four distinct forms of teaching can be distinguished – exposition or directive teaching; discussion; action or experiential learning; and enquiry/problem solving. On this view the skilled teacher is someone who has acquired the ability to use each of these four modes to good effect and can make informed judgments about their deployment in relation to educational aims and teaching contexts (CCC, 1983:46).

The MacFarlane report rightly drew attention to the importance of helping students, through their higher education experience, to develop effective communication skills, problem-solving and collaborative group work skills (MacFarlane, 1992: 4). These are precisely the kinds of skills that would be developed through a balanced application of the four modes of teaching. Discussion and enquiry are not only teaching methods through which students gain important disciplined understanding: they are also important in demonstrating to students how to discuss effectively and how to enquire, whether in history, religion, economics or whatever. Entwistle points out that in future we need to consider

> not the effectiveness of a method of teaching to improve the general quality of learning but the ways in which each available method might contribute to each of the specific skills expected to be developed in a particular course. (Entwistle, 1993:13).

It is our contention that the idea of teaching modes is helpful here in drawing attention to basic forms of teaching which have distinctive strengths of this kind. The modes theory can provide an overall conceptual framework within which more detailed distinctions might be developed in order to identify appropriate teaching practices and priorities for staff development.

A second aspect of the MacFarlane analysis is the identification of phases of learning for 'thorough conceptual understanding' (MacFarlane, 1992: 6). The report asks how far each of the various traditional teaching methods, lecture, tutorial, practical, etc., matches a particular phase or phases of learning. However, it is important to note that such an analysis can only deal with structured conceptual learning. It will not cover experiential learning or the now common enquiry-based final year projects; nor will it readily link with the diverse ways in which students are motivated to the study of particular disciplines and get on the inside of particular forms of knowledge and understanding.

This issue has been further discussed by Entwistle (Entwistle, 1993), who considers these traditional categories of teaching in terms of specific objectives such as concepts, detailed knowledge, conceptual understanding, writing cogently, problem-solving, co-operative learning, and computer skills. This is a promising approach and our argument is that it would be strengthened by a clearer conception of different kinds of teaching.

Traditional categories like practicals, tutorials, or small group work are no longer satisfactory for they hide a multitude of different teaching processes under a single term. It is never clear how far these overlap. Are lectures not often given to small groups? How does independent study link to lectures? What different forms of small group work is it useful to distinguish? Above all, there is little power in the analysis of these as forms of teaching. They also fail to draw on the benefits from research in other sectors of education such as Dillon's work on discussion at secondary school level (Dillon, 1988), Bennett's work on collaborative group work in the primary school (Bennett and Dunne, 1992), and theories of adult learning (Thorpe et al, 1993).

These traditional categories have never been seriously examined for their usefulness in the current phase of the development of teaching in higher education. It is not obvious that they are the most useful terms or that they give the kind of analytic power that is required for the effective development of teaching. *Analysis tends to be in terms of student learning rather than teaching interactions, teaching structures and teaching rationales.* There has been considerable attention to conceptions of student learning but not a parallel analysis of conceptions of higher education teaching methods.

What needs to be asked, surely, is not what can practicals or tutorials contribute but what role does experiential learning or enquiry learning have? What could genuine discussions (as opposed to many typical tutorials) contribute to the course objectives? What direct (i.e. expository) teaching is required, whether through lecture, textbook or video? This would surely be a more powerful analytic approach and provide a useful basis for evaluating teaching methods on a particular course and for considering staff development needs.

The modes concept has a considerable but unrealised potential. It provides a simple, balanced, open, flexible and powerful approach to making sense of the variety of teaching. It cuts through the false dichotomy of traditional/innovative and identifies a range of approaches to teaching adequate to the wide-ranging aims and contexts of higher education today. Its power lies in the claim to identify four fundamentally different ways of teaching and the implication that each mode demands distinctive organisation, resources and teaching skills. Thinking in terms of teaching modes quickly takes one to the key teaching issues and to consideration of the links between aims, structures and teaching skills. Unfortunately, pedagogical discussion has been dominated by the search for the *one best way* or the supposed general characteristics of effective teaching (Silcock, 1993, Ramsden, 1992) or the dismissal of teaching in favour of learning. This has inhibited proper discussion of the distinctive features of each mode and its associated skills in many discussions of higher education learning as of school education.

There is much development work to be done on teaching modes: activity (action and experiential) learning is perhaps best conceived as a cycle of planning, doing and reflecting (Weil and McGill, 1989), for what is learned through activity depends crucially on the quality of the thinking involved. Discussion needs to be distinguished from the essentially expository 'question and answer' to which it is so often reduced (Dillon, 1988, 1994, Bridges, 1979); and the enquiry mode needs to come to terms with the debate about how far problem-solving is a general as opposed to a discipline-specific skill, and what structure for effective enquiry learning can be developed (Hennessy *et al*, 1993). Exposition needs to be modernised to match a constructivist perspective on learning (Von Glaserfeld, 1986, Gibbs, 1992), and information technology developments need to be acted upon (Wood, 1993). However, the basic notion of the four modes of teaching has proved a fruitful one in primary and secondary education. The initial evidence from a Moray House staff development initiative on teaching and learning, which is based on the four modes concept, is that it can prove equally fruitful in relation to higher education teaching and staff development.

The Development of Flexible and Open Learning

One of the Institute's principal methods of promoting innovation in teaching and learning is the Quality of Student Learning Initiative (QUOSLI) which began in session 1989-90. It was established with the aim of promoting approaches to teaching and learning which might be subsumed under the terms 'flexible learning' or 'open learning'. Such approaches aim at increasing student autonomy in learning and have some or all of the following characteristics

- students are given increased responsibility for their own work
- students can progress at a pace which suits their needs
- students learn from their peers and from reflecting on their own experience
- there is increased access for students to learning resources
- there is a greater degree of student choice
- learning can take place in a number of locations.

Staffing and related resources are provided to enable departments to design and implement a teaching project which can be monitored and evaluated before any large scale dissemination. The focus of development has varied from year to year. In 1991/92 the focus was on developing materials for cross–college modules and in 1992/93 it was on developing student materials for the MA (TESOL) by distance learning programme. Staff are supported by the Institute's Senior Lecturer (Open Learning), who has compiled a Handbook for the use of those involved in producing materials.

The most common products of the various schemes supported by the QUOSLI initiative are packs of materials designed to support students, whether studying on their own or with a tutor. In the case of the former, these materials enable students to work at a time, place and pace of their own choosing. In some cases materials to assist staff are also developed.

The range of projects supported by QUOSLI is illustrated by the following examples :-

- self-study materials for the cross-college first-year undergraduate Information Technology module
- a guide to the extended study for students on the Institute's Master's level programmes
- development of multi-media materials (CDi) for the cross-college module on Equal Opportunities.

In the area of in-service education for teachers, Moray House has played a part in developing and delivering mixed-mode (part distance learning, part centre-based) materials for the SOED 'Management Training for Headteachers' initiative. With colleagues from other colleges and faculties of education, Moray House staff have also been involved in the development of distance learning materials such as those used in the Certificate in Primary Environmental Education. The advantages of such an approach to in-service education is that teachers can experiment with the ideas in the materials in their own schools or classrooms, reflect on these experiences and discuss them with their colleagues at subsequent meetings. Materials embodying similar ideas have been devised for technology staff in secondary schools preparing for the introduction of a new course in technological studies.

One of the Institute's most interesting innovations is the MA (TESOL) by distance learning programme, which is being developed by staff in the Institute's Scottish Centre for International Education. In comparison with the materials described previously this is an innovation in three respects :-

- it is at Master's level
- it is aimed at students who are not based in the UK
- although some of the Units may be taken in Moray House, the course is designed to be wholly distance learning.

This innovation was developed partly to provide access to Moray House expertise in the field of English language teaching by a wider range of students and partly in response to a change of direction in the British Government's aid policy. It is a good example of the kind of flexible approach to teaching which has the capability of helping higher education institutions to meet many of the challenges that lie ahead.

Information Technology in Support of Teaching and Learning

The application of information technology (IT) to support effective and efficient teaching and learning in higher education is a rapidly expanding field both in terms of new developments and of research projects. The Institute's IT policy recognises that

> *the quality of teaching and learning can be enhanced by appropriate uses of IT.* (Academic Board, 1993).

The MacFarlane Report provided a detailed overview of the types of applications of IT to teaching in higher education. Whilst the Institute welcomed the report, there was concern at the suggested establishment of national structures to co-ordinate, commission and disseminate 'shareable resources'. Evidence on the impact of previous major national development projects does not suggest that such 'top down' initiatives achieve their objectives. Such an approach is even less likely to succeed in a field as rapidly evolving as information technology. Technological considerations, particularly where these are bound up in discussions about efficiency, should not lead to inappropriate pedagogical decisions. Professional judgments as to when a specific computer-based technique is appropriate should continue to be made only in relation to the learning outcomes involved.

One of the national developments reflecting increasing interest in IT applications was the setting up of the first phase of the Teaching and Learning Technology Programme in 1992 by the then Universities Funding Council. This programme aimed to

> *. . . make teaching and learning more productive and efficient by harnessing modern technology.* (UFC, 1992).

In 1993 the new higher education funding councils agreed to jointly support phase two of this programme bringing the total number of funded projects across the UK to 76.

In Moray House the strategy has been to support a variety of IT developments through its Quality of Student Learning Initiative. Thus, for the common undergraduate module in Information Technology, text-based core units were created and piloted, students being provided with supported self-study materials. Apple Macintosh hardware and software were made available via Open Access computer workshops. Because of the variety of competences and understanding that first-year undergraduates bring with them the remaining part of the module was developed as a series of self-study option units. Student evaluation was very positive, with high levels of confidence about all aspects of IT being recorded.

Another project reflects a different type of IT application. A second-year undergraduate common module is concerned with aspects of Equal Opportunities and the enhancement of students' anti-discriminatory perceptions. The majority of the teaching involves problem-solving discussion groups. However, the module team is currently planning and producing, with the support of the Institute's multi-media producer and ETV Unit, a CDi programme. This will enable students to work in small groups and consider a variety of case studies highlighting key equal opportunities issues. This project is also being used to test some of the principal pedagogical ideas associated with such interactive multi-media technologies. These include the application of the interactive facilities of CDi, the enhancement of student choice, the facilitating of students' working at a time and place of their own choosing, and the development of problem-solving through the evaluation of 'what if' or 'what next' scenarios.

At the Cramond campus an Interactive Video Disc (IV) is being developed on the theme of Scottish Traditional Dance. Staff are also applying, in a variety of contexts, the IV disc produced to support the staff development programme associated with the Revised Higher in Physical Education.

The Institute recognises the enormous potential for supporting teaching and learning through the application of IT. However, there are no simple solutions: no single technology that can provide an adequate solution to the complexities involved in teaching in higher education. Similarly, the rapid changes in technology suggest that in the medium term a gradualist, experimental approach should be adopted rather than a central revolutionary model. However, there is an important national role which can be identified concerned with the dissemination of successful innovations, particularly where these can be adapted to the specific requirements of departments and institutions. The development of the Super JANET network, with its facilities for the rapid transmission of text, graphics and video, represents an exciting tool for the exchange of teaching ideas across the UK and world-wide.

Monitoring Teaching and Learning

Moray House has a history of accountability to the professional bodies that recognise its qualifications (the General Teaching Council (GTC), the Central Council for the Education and Training of Social Workers (CCETSW), and the Scottish Community Education Council (SCEC)), to the SOED, to the CNNA until 1992 for the validation of degrees and currently to Heriot-Watt University. For this reason it has always recognised the importance of regular monitoring and the evaluation of teaching and learning.

The Institute has established a number of procedures for monitoring teaching and learning and we describe five types of institutional accountability.

1. Monitoring by **Module Co-ordinators** and their teaching teams to ensure that the academic content of modules is of high quality and that teaching methods are appropriate to the learning outcomes. This is based on **individual lecturers** providing high quality teaching based on an understanding of learning theory and scholarship in their academic specialism. A module evaluation questionnaire is routinely completed by students at the end of each module as the standard mechanism for assessing students' perceptions of 'quality'. Completed questionnaires are optically read and summary statistics computed for use by module co-ordinators and course leaders.

2. **Course Leader** monitoring to ensure that the overall programme leading to an award meets the stated learning outcomes and that the programme is regularly evaluated and reviewed by the appropriate course committee.

3. **Directorial** monitoring ensures that the learning outcomes of all the courses/modules within a programme area, such as teaching, or social work, or community education, meet the standards and expectations of the appropriate professional bodies, and that appropriate links with employers and field professionals are maintained.

4. **Institutional** monitoring concerns the analysis of the range, nature, standard and cost effectiveness of courses and modules. Such monitoring involves decisions about staffing levels, resources, assessment procedures, course duration and procedures relating to external examiners. At Moray House this work is done mainly by the Academic Board and the Academic Standards Committee.

5. **External** monitoring involves the scrutiny of new courses or modules, the external validation of new programmes and modules, and the periodic review of these programmes by external bodies such as the GTC, SOED, CNNA, SCEC and CCETSW. It also involves the use of the external examining system in which people with authority from other institutions and professional bodies scrutinise the standards achieved. Finally, there is a further layer of external monitoring through the work of the quality assessment and quality audit agencies, which are described in Chapter 10.

Of the five types of accountability the last four are concerned largely with the monitoring of *written* criteria for effective teaching and learning. Only the first deals with face to face contact with students, and an immediate concern with teaching methods on the part of the individual lecturer. Whilst the course structure and module descriptor will outline the main parameters for teaching and learning, it is usually the case that teaching methods are outlined in a way that provide academic staff with considerable freedom.

Staff Development for Teaching and Learning

The Moray House Staff Development Policy includes the following statements:

> *Staff development should lead directly or indirectly to the improvement of teaching, research, consultancy and student learning in the Institute and to the enhancement of the professional activities fostered by the institution.*

> *Staff development has an important part to play in maintaining individual job satisfaction, enhancing the ability of staff to achieve the objectives of the Institute and enabling the Institute to respond to rapid social, technological and educational change.*

In many higher education institutions teaching methodology has until recently rarely been the subject of formal discussion. Indeed, with staff development in British universities still in its infancy, some staff still see it as a strictly personal activity, requiring only funding (for conferences) and time (for research and scholarship) from their employer. Interviews with university staff suggest that staff development often concerns subject knowledge rather than teaching methods and that whilst courses are regularly reviewed such reviews often ignore teaching methods. It is assumed that individual lecturers are responsible for the quality of their own teaching.

A major focus of staff development at Moray House is the individual lecturer, the aim being to enable and empower academic staff to take control of their own professional development. Workshops and seminars are normally offered during specific 'staff development days', which are centrally time-tabled to enable Institute staff to give priority to them at points throughout the academic year. As part of that programme of staff development, the Institute currently operates a research forum, an IT forum and a teaching and learning forum based on the growing practice of 'reflective action' in higher education teaching.

Staff development has in, recent years, highlighted teaching and learning, and an analysis of staff development seminars and workshops confirms the wide variety of opportunities for academic staff to discuss teaching methods in higher education. For example, Moray House-funded research (McMichael and Garry, 1991) on the supervision of dissertations led to the production of a handbook dealing with the role of the supervisor, the structure of supervision and institutional support, a guide to training workshops and a video. The researchers have conducted a number of training sessions for staff on project supervision within the Institute's staff development programme. In addition to the induction programme for new staff there are further opportunities for experienced staff to develop their teaching skills. Since 1993 a 'Reflective Action Programme' has been developed comprising five monthly workshops linked to a programme of action research into the participants' own teaching and using the four modes of teaching as its conceptual framework.

Staff development, with its focus on the professional skills of academic staff, has developed various methods to encourage the more widespread consideration of teaching methods. In a relatively small institution, where academic staff meet one another fairly often, staff development can operate in a more organic way than is the case in larger institutions. Discussion about teaching methods is important and staff development can facilitate this. However, the first stage in improving the practice of academic staff is that they *become aware of what they actually do*. For this reason the 1993/ 94 Reflective Action Course is a small but important step towards improving practice.

Conclusion

The development of effective teaching and learning in higher education requires an appropriate institutional response to external influences and pressures, an understanding of the range of teaching methods currently employed, an appropriate staff development programme based on recent research and classroom-based teacher research, an induction programme for new academic staff to include training in teaching methods and a system for the development of teaching materials. All of these developments are taking place at Moray House. In addition, whereas in many institutions what happens in the lecture theatre or seminar room may be shrouded in mystery, increasingly at Moray House academic staff are creating a climate of team-teaching, shared informal peer evaluation, and teaching and learning is a key feature of academic and professional exchange.

As to the future, the likely impact of information technology is not yet completely clear. The roles of multi-media in support of student learning; the changes to information access brought about by world-wide networks, and the enhancement of all forms of communication cannot be clearly predicted. However, the opportunities offered will be fully grasped in order to support our students' learning.

References

Academic Board, (1993). Moray House Academic Board paper.

Bain, W. H. (1985). 'The Historical Perspective', in Kirk, G. (Ed.), *Moray House and Professional Education 1835-1985*, Edinburgh, Scottish Academic Press.

Bennett, N. and Dunne, E. (1992). 'Managing Classroom Groups', London, Simon and Schuster.

Bennett, N. and Carre, C. (1993). *Learning to Teach*. Routledge, London.

Bridges, D. (1979). *Education, Democracy and Discussions*. NFER, Slough.

Carr, D. (1992). 'Practical Enquiry, Values and the Problem of Educational Theory', *Oxford Review of Education*, Vol. 18, No. 3, pp. 241-251.

Carr, D. (1993). 'Guidelines for Teacher Training : the Competency Model', *Scottish Educational Review*, 25, pp. 17-25.

Carr, D. (1994). 'Educational Enquiry and Professional Knowledge: Towards a Copernican Revolution', *Educational Studies*, Vol. 20, No. 1, pp. 33-52.

CCC, COPE (1983). 'Primary Education in the Eighties', Dundee, CCC.

Cosford, B.D., McNie, R. and Skinner, D. (1993) 'Quality in Learning and Teaching – an Interim Report', (Moray House internal research report).

Dillon, J. (1988). *Questioning and Teaching,* Croom Helm, London.

Dillon, J. (1994). *Using Discussion in Classrooms*, Open University Press, Buckingham.

Entwistle, N. (1993). 'Future Directions in Research into Teaching and Learning in Higher Education', paper presented to SCRE Workshop: Towards a Research Programme on Teaching and Learning in Higher Education in Scotland, March 1993.

Entwistle, N. (1992). 'The Impact of Teaching on Learning Outcomes in Higher Education – A Literature Review', CVCP/USDU.

Entwistle, N. and Tait, H. (1992). 'Approaches to Learning, Evaluations of Teaching and Preferences for Contrasting Academic Environments', Higher Education, 19, pp. 169-194.

Gibbs, G. (1992). 'Improving the Quality of Student Learning', Technical and Educational Services Ltd.

Hall, J. and Black, H. (1993). 'Workshop Discussion' in 'Towards a Research Programme on Teaching and Learning in Higher Education in Scotland': Proceedings of an Invitational Workshop at the Scottish Council for Research in Education to discuss the report Teaching and Learning in higher education, SCRE, March 1993.

Hennessy, S. McCormick, R. and Murchy, P. 'The Myth of General Problem Solving Capability: Design and Technology as an Example', Curriculum Journal, Vol. 4, No. 1, pp. 73-90.

Kirk, G. (1984). 'The New BEd in Scotland: Towards a Professional Degree', Scottish Educational Review, Vol. 16, No. 1, pp. 19-26.

Kirk, G. (Ed.) (1985). *Moray House and Professional Education 1835-1985*, Scottish Academic Press, Edinburgh.

Kirk, G. (1988). 'The Professionalisation of Teaching and its Frustration', Scottish Educational Review, Vol. 20, No. 1, pp. 1-21.

Laurillard, D. (1993). *Rethinking University Teaching*, Routledge, London.

MacFarlane Report (1992). 'Teaching and Learning in an Expanding Higher Education System', The Committee of the Scottish University Principals.

McMichael, P. and Garry, A. (1991). 'Strategies for Supervision', Moray House Institute of Education, Edinburgh.

MacNamara, D. (1994). *Classroom Pedagogy and Primary Practice*, Routledge, London.

Marton, F., Dall'Alba, G., and Beaty, E. (1992). 'Conceptions of Learning', International Journal of Educational Research, p. 14.

Peacock, C. (1990). *Classroom Skills in English Teaching'*, Routledge, London.

Ramsden, P. (1992). *Learning to Teach in Higher Education,* Routledge, London.

SED (1983). 'Guidelines for Teacher Training', SED, Edinburgh.

SED (1985). 'Guidelines on Learning and Teaching Approaches 16+', SED, Edinburgh.

SHEFC, (1993) Scottish Higher Education Funding Council Circular Letter 64/93, 24 December 1993.

Shulman, (1986). 'Paradigms and Research programmes in the Study of Teaching: a contemporary Perspective', in Whittrock, M. C. (Ed.) Handbook of Research in Teaching, 3rd edn, Macmillan, New York.

Silcock, P. (1993). 'Can We Teach Effective Teaching?' Educational Review, Vol. 45, No. 1, pp. 13-19

Thorpe, G. *et al.* (1993). *Culture and Processes of Adult Learning*, Routledge, London.

UFC, (1992). Universities Funding Council Circular 8/92.

Von Glaserfeld, E. (1987). 'Learning as a Constructive Activity', in Janner, C. (Ed.) Problems of Representation in Teaching and Learning of Mathematics.

Weil, S. W. and McGill, I. (1989). *Making Sense of Experiential Learning*, SRHE/Open University, Buckingham.

Wood, D. (1993). 'The Classroom of 2015', National Commission on Education Briefing No. 20, Paul Hamlyn, London.

9

Research

Hugh E. Perfect

In 1985, institutions like Moray House received funds to support research activity from the Scottish Education Department. The staffing entitlement of colleges of education included an 8% allowance for research and development work. In addition, each year the SED placed funds with the National Inter-College Committee for Educational Research (NICCER), and individual institutions competed for a share of these funds by making bids for research projects. That form of funding was supplemented by an annual discretionary grant from the SED to enable college staff to mount small-scale feasibility studies. These various forms of support were attempts by the SED to establish a research base in the colleges of education and to enable them to play a more prominent role in research alongside the universities, where research was much more securely established, and Scotland's national research agency, the Scottish Council for Educational Research.

The public support for research activity helped Moray House to expand its research activities and in *Moray House and Professional Education,* Wilson and Perfect (1985) in their review of the Institute's research activities referred to 'the improvement in the status of research in Moray House over the past 20 years'. However, they concluded that there was 'scope for further enquiry into how far research had become part of the woodwork of the institution'. Ten years on, what does that further enquiry demonstrate?

There have been dramatic changes in the national arrangements for funding research since 1985. From 1987 the support provided annually by the SED was discontinued and the generous staffing allowance withdrawn, notwithstanding the recommendation in the STEAC report that colleges of education, like the central institutions, should receive funds to support research work. The effect of these changes was to place the colleges of education in open competition with their more generously funded colleagues in the universities for research money. Now, each year the Scottish Office Education Department, after undertaking its internal trawl of research needs, identifies research priorities and places a limited number of projects, usually about six, with institutions after a carefully arranged but keenly competitive tendering system. Bids are assessed in relation to public criteria and contracts placed accordingly. Colleges of education have lost whatever sheltered support they received and must now flourish in a fiercely competitive research environment.

There has been a second major change in the context of research. With the establishment of the Scottish Higher Education Funding Council and the repatriation of the Scottish universities, a common approach to funding for teaching and for research has been adopted. All institutions of higher education, irrespective of designation, are subject to the same procedures and the application of the same formula for funding. The allocation of funds for teaching relate to the number of students attracted, with provision made for different categories of course. A standard unit of resource is computed and that provides the basis for the financial allocation. Provision for funds for research is determined by a nationwide evaluation of the quality of research conducted by institutions, the Research Assessment Exercise. Moray House entered this UK-wide research assessment for the first time in 1992 and had its work assessed in the same way as that of other institutions. In the new context it is, of course, no longer possible for institutions to rely purely on past reputations; and no longer can the maintenance of the current research position be the objective: the enhancement of quality and scale compared to other institutions must now be the goal.

Partly as a consequence of these changes in the national funding arrangements, research has now become one of Moray House's central preoccupations alongside teaching and consultancy. Naturally, given its history and its place in higher education in Scotland, teaching is Moray House's predominant activity. A recent document affirmed the institution's position in these words:

> It is the direct engagement with students that is the first and most important responsibility of staff, and it is that engagement which is the primary source of their satisfaction and achievement, as well as their sense of professional identity: first and foremost they are teachers. (Moray House, 1994).

Without weakening that commitment to teaching, the Institute has also, over the last decade, established itself as a centre for consultancy. Its standing in this field derives from its role as a major provider of in-service education and support for practising professionals in post, and from the involvement of staff in a wide range of national and local development programmes. That involvement places Moray House staff in the forefront of developments in its acknowledged areas of professional expertise and means that staff are in very considerable demand in a variety of professional contexts to share their expertise and to offer support for development work of various kinds. Chapter 12 of this volume analyses the growth of this feature of the Institute's work.

Of course, teaching and consultancy share a common base and that is the professional expertise of staff. Just as the skills of teaching can transfer easily and naturally to a range of consultancy contexts, so engagement in consultancy work with groups of professionals can revitalise teaching, enhance credibility, and enrich the intellectual climate of an institution. The same may be said of engagement in research. One of the key features of the CNAA approach to course validation was the requirement that those involved in teaching degree programmes should themselves engage in research or some form of scholarly activity. Teaching that cannot draw on fresh knowledge and insights is arid; and over the years the substantial increase in the involvement of staff on research work rested at least partly on the belief that good teaching presupposes a secure and expanding knowledge base provided by research activity.

Indeed, there would be something hollow about Moray House's claim to be a major centre of professional education if it regarded itself merely as an institution for communicating knowledge and understanding: it has to accept its obligation to generate knowledge and understanding, and it does that by making research feature as one of its three central preoccupations. Naturally, the changes effected by the 1992 legislation and the Research Assessment Exercise serve to reinforce the emergence of research as a fundamental institutional imperative.

The 1992 Research Assessment Exercise

The 1992 exercise was the third to be conducted on a national basis. Its purpose was to provide advice to enable the higher education funding councils to allocate funds on a selective basis as required by the government. It was characterised by an open approach with all institutions being consulted on the framework and procedures to be adopted.

The exercise was based on informed peer review by a number of specialist panels. Panels were set up for each of the 72 Units of Assessment into which the research effort of UK higher education was categorised, with membership based on the criterion of pre-eminence in research. Institutions were invited to provide evidence about their research efforts in the form of two publications and up to two other forms of public output for each member of staff identified as an 'active researcher'. Panels also had access to other information including research grant and contract income and the number of research-related staff such as research assistants. Clearly, the exercise was a major undertaking and, by the closing date of 30 June 1992, some 2,700 submissions had been received from 170 higher education institutions across the 72 Units of Assessment. The work of over 45,000 full-time equivalent academics was included in these submissions.

Each institutional submission to a Unit of Assessment was given a quality rating. The ratings ranged from 5, representing work which had attained a level of international excellence in some areas and national excellence in virtually all others, to 1, representing a level of national excellence in virtually no area of work. Moray House submitted work in three Units of Assessment: Education, Social Work, and Physical Education and Sports Science. The Education area represented the most substantial submission with 37 staff classified as active researchers. A very creditable rating of three was achieved. Across the UK the old universities obtained an average quality rating of 3.76; the new universities and colleges averaged 1.96. Drawing on the findings of the Research Assessment Exercise, SHEFC allocated to Scottish institutions funding which required to be dedicated to supporting research activities. Based on the quality rating achieved and the number of active researchers SHEFC awarded Moray House the second highest level of funding in the Education subject. For the financial year 1994/95 this amounted to £487,000. The Institute also received research funds for developmental and pump-priming purposes amounting to £45,000.

Research and the Strategic Plan

The nature of research at Moray House demands a long term planning horizon and continuing commitment. The Institute's mission statement highlights research as a central concern:

> . . . to contribute to human understanding of how professional practice is to be enhanced . . . and . . . to conduct research and development work.

The aim of the Institute's strategy is to enhance both the quality and extent of its research activities in absolute and comparative terms. The focus for research activities continues to be the three areas submitted in 1992 viz: Education, Social Work, and Physical Education and Leisure Studies. Each area has identified a number of priorities. For example, in Education these include:

- research into aspects of higher education, including mentoring, teaching and learning, and quality assurance
- professional career development, including the experience of probationary teachers and social workers
- aspects of special educational needs
- Community Education, including adult and life long learning
- curricular issues such as values education and health education
- educational management
- the application of interactive technologies to teaching and staff development.

The Research Committee

The committee plays an important role in facilitating the research activities of the Holyrood and Cramond campuses. It disseminates information to researchers and provides a forum for debating key issues. Where appropriate it undertakes a peer evaluation of new research projects submitted by staff and appoints a link member to newly approved projects. It also supports the provision of staff development opportunities, particularly for staff who wish to develop research skills.

The committee monitors the research programme of the Institute and provides the Academic Board with an annual evaluation report. However, the Committee recognises the long-term nature of the research enterprise and consequently monitoring is intentionally at arms length: the principal evaluation of the work of Institute's researchers will be by its reception by other professionals and through the Research Assessment Exercises.

A working group of the committee is responsible for the arrangements for matriculating, supervising and examining post graduate research students. The Institute's procedures are consistent with those of the Post-Graduate Studies Committee of Heriot Watt University and the degrees awarded are those of the University. There has been a steady increase in the number of part-time research students over the past two years and increasing interest from overseas students in undertaking educational research at Moray House. With this increase in students has come the need to involve more staff in a supervisory role since each degree student has access to a first and second supervisor. To satisfy this need a series of meetings has taken place between supervisors and potential supervisors, and a training programme has been initiated.

In the light of that formal commitment to research, how is the enhanced importance of research reflected in the life of the institution? It is reflected, first of all, in the increased involvement of staff in research. When the Scottish Office discontinued its practice of granting colleges of education an 8% allowance for research and development, Moray House continued to 'top-slice' funds from its own resources in order to protect the involvement of staff in research. Over the years, between fifteen and eighteen full-time equivalent staff were allocated to research. That staffing allowance is managed by the Research Committee, which approves projects and apportions staff time for research accordingly. As a result of that policy, a substantial proportion of staff – just under 50% in the present year – are engaged on formally approved Moray House research projects.

Of course, the formal protection of staff time for research activity depends on other forms of institutional support. Accordingly, the Institute has attempted to control time devoted to teaching by varying the students' formal class contact time as the overall SSR has deteriorated. The thinking behind this policy is to ensure that, important though direct engagement with students undoubtedly is, its quality depends on the quality of work undertaken by staff when they are not directly involved in teaching.

Staff are also supported in their research work by research seminars, by staff development activities of various kinds, including financial support in working for higher degrees, by the provision of opportunity to discuss research findings and problems, and by providing an avenue for dissemination of research reports through Moray House publications. The creation of these various forms of support is the responsibility of two senior lecturers for research, one on each campus, who seek to foster research across the institution under the overall responsibility of the Senior Assistant Principal.

Secondly, the Institute seeks to enhance its research profile through recruitment. The plan is to appoint one or two distinguished researchers each year at professorial level through the University's procedures. These professors will, of course, be expected to conduct research and lead bids for research funds, but will also help to develop teams of staff who engage in research on a collaborative basis. In addition, one of the criteria used in all academic staff appointments at Moray House now is evidence of engagement in research and development activities. That recruitment policy, allied to the protection of staff time for research and other staff development activities, should mean that, in the years ahead, all academic staff at Moray House will be involved in research and all will be registrable as 'active researchers'.

The third main feature of the Institute's research strategy is to give high priority to research in teaching. As part of the Institute's modularisation strategy, all undergraduates take a compulsory module on Research and Enquiry in the Social Sciences. The purpose of that unit is two-fold: to enable and encourage students to use the periodical literature; and to prepare them to conduct investigations into their own professional activities. All undergraduates at Moray House are required to complete a major dissertation as the culminating phase of their studies. That takes the form of a professional report of work undertaken, analysed and evaluated in a school or some other setting. For their part, all students embarking on the postgraduate Modular Master's Programme are required to take the postgraduate research module and, again, the final phase of study for the degree is a major research dissertation. The research emphasis of undergraduate and postgraduate programmes, the latter offering some twenty different pathways, has encouraged the growth in the number of research students and research assistants. All of these developments have provided a substantial impetus to the creation of a research culture at Moray House. One of the signs of that culture is that the Institute now has sufficient strength in research to mount a Master's Degree Programme in Social and Educational Research.

The fourth feature of the Institute's approach to research is the adoption of a strategy for research. Given the size of the institution, it would be inappropriate to spread research efforts too widely: Moray House needs to concentrate on its strengths and to build on these. These are the areas in which professorial appointments are being made and where resources require to be concentrated, with the aim of building for Moray House a national and international reputation. The following areas of concentration have been identified:

(a) **The Centre for Leisure Research (CLR):** Based at the Cramond Campus, the CLR has established itself as a leading research establishment which has a successful track record of bidding for external funds. In 1993/94 in excess of £350,000 was won in an increasingly competitive environment. The Director of CLR, Fred Coalter, also plays a wider role at the Cramond Campus as Senior Lecturer (Research) with responsibility for facilitating and supporting the overall research programme.

(b) **The Scottish Interactive Technology Centre (SITC):** SITC has been, and is currently, engaged in the design, production and development of interactive video and CDi multi-media resources to support school-based staff development activities in both primary and secondary sectors. This work has been carried out on behalf of SOED, the Department of Environment, and others, and has produced a series of resources which are being widely used in Scotland and the rest of the UK. A significant feature of the work involves research, by Tony van der Kuyl and Byron

Evans, into the most appropriate teaching and learning styles which can be supported and enhanced through the application of multi-media technologies.

(c) **Placement and Mentoring:** Professor Margot Cameron-Jones has led a series of research studies extending over 20 years which focus on the ways in which professional skills and knowledge are fostered during placement. That research has been particularly concerned with the enhanced role of professionals in training. When the Scottish Office Education Department decided to introduce a pilot project on mentoring in the secondary school, the responsibility for the project was placed with Moray House, partly in recognition of that research tradition.

(d) **Special Educational Needs:** A wide range of research and development activities has been undertaken within the area of special educational needs, funded by the Scottish Office Education Department and other agencies. Marianna Buultjens has analysed extensive video material of young blind children at play; Margaret Lee has engaged in evaluating different approaches to orientation and mobility training for pupils with multiple learning difficulties; Alison Closs has researched the educational provision of two hitherto marginal groups of pupils within the Czech Republic – Gypsy children and those with severe/profound and complex learning difficulties; Fernando Diniz has undertaken work into ethnic minorities and special education; Gwynedd Lloyd has been concerned with the emotional and behavioural difficulties associated with the reintegration into mainstream schools; and, finally, Judith Watson has undertaken a major study of pupils with moderate learning difficulties.

(e) **Professional Development:** Janet Draper, Helen Fraser and Warwick Taylor have collaborated for many years on a major follow-up study of teacher probationers and are continuing that longitudinal study with support from the Scottish Office Education Department and the General Teaching Council. Paquita McMichael and Janet Draper have undertaken a study of staff in institutions of higher education on secondment or on fixed-term contracts. David Turner, Ian Knowles, Janet Draper and Jim Kidd have been concerned with the impact of the National Headteacher Management Training modules on the management of change in Lothian schools.

(f) **Institutional Research:** Stephen Sharp and Pat McLaughlin have led a programme of research into aspects of the Institute's own educational effectiveness. That has involved a study of course evaluation, of non-completion rates, and of the Institute's selection arrangements. Part of that programme of research has involved a study of teaching and learning and has been undertaken by Brian Cosford, Don Skinner, and Bob McNie.

(g) **Community Education:** Research in community education has several main strands: to consider how theories in use by practitioners and policy-makers impact on provision; to examine how participation in community education by disadvantaged groups can be increased; and to explore issues and concerns facing practitioners, such as anti-racist and anti-sexist approaches, environmental education, and student progression.

External Grants

With the demise of NICCER, and the move by the SOED to seek competitive tenders for its priority research projects, the obtaining of external research grants has become increasingly competitive. The Institute has had increasing success in winning grants and currently is in receipt of funds from the Scottish Office Education Department, the Economic and Social Research Council, the Scottish Higher Education Funding Council, Lothian Health Board and the Waverley Care Trust, the Department of the Environment, EIS/University Lecturers' Association, and the Health Education Board for Scotland. Since one of the criteria used in the assessment of research in an institution of higher education is its capacity to attract external funding, it is clearly of considerable importance that the Institute continues to attract funding from such bodies.

Publications and Dissemination

At the heart of the Institute's research enterprise is the need to publish findings and to submit work to the scrutiny of academic and professional peers. If a criticism could be levelled previously it is that the process of research was valued more highly than the public reporting of what had been achieved. Only by publishing, in its widest sense, can research be scrutinized by other researchers and so become part of the wider understanding of the educational community. Research, whilst a highly creative individual or team enterprise, derives real significance through publication and public discussion. The Moray House Publications Unit has been established to foster publication and is responsible for a growing number of books and research reports by academic staff.

The Way Ahead

Despite the scale and comprehensiveness of the last Research Assessment Exercise and its associated financial implications, the procedures were broadly recognised as the best that could be realistically achieved without devoting significantly more resources. It has been calculated that the Research Assessment Exercise cost in the region of £13.5 million, which, however, represents less than 0.5% of the value of the funding which the Exercise helps to allocate.

The concept of peer review is considered to be a central feature of any such system and there is widespread support for the UK-wide context. A number of the detailed issues of the RAE raised by the Research Committee are shared by the higher education system as a whole. The method of selecting the membership of the panels for each Unit of Assessment, to ensure their credibility, is crucial as is the early publication of the criteria to be used to adjudge quality. The means of establishing rating five might also be considered problematic unless a panel had access to international membership.

The nature of the evidence upon which panels make their quality judgements has been subject to extensive discussion. There is a shared view that the RAE's principal purpose is the determination of quality, not productivity. The 1992 Exercise included information for each active researcher on the total number and type of research output alongside the four selected key pieces of work. An emphasis on quantity could have unfortunate effects on publication behaviour. *The process of collecting and publishing data will have a behavioural effect, especially if it is used to influence funding.* (Joint Performance Indicators Working Group, 1994). The decision to drop the overall quantitative element from the 1996 RAE is therefore to be welcomed. An analysis of the 1992 RAE confirms that some quantitative measurements contain a qualitative element. For example, there was a strong correlation between academic journal articles and research ratings across a wide range of Units of Assessment. Other types of product, such as conference papers, books and other products, were more relevant to some subjects than others.

A growing debate centres on the issue of research priorities. SHEFC has already flagged the possibility of introducing a factor – the 'priority weighting factor' – into its funding formula. It can be argued that the establishment of priorities should be left to the strategic planning of individual institutions which will take into account national and international factors in their planning process. The question remains as to whether SHEFC will consider the sum total of institutional priorities to be sufficient and whether this policy will be acceptable to the Council's paymaster – the government. National priorities would undoubtedly become equated with governmental ones and in this case the long-term research effort of institutions might be influenced detrimentally by short-term ministerial expediency.

However, a national discussion about research priorities might enable consideration to be given to those Units of Assessment which clearly reflect underdeveloped yet important research areas. For example, in Scotland the Physical Education and Sports Science field achieved a single two rating and two ratings of one. This level of quality achievement leads in turn to restricted SHEFC funding, generating a circle of continuing under-investment. The converse to this argument is one which would value most highly those national centres of excellence with successful track records. Whatever the outcome of this debate, which may in the end be decided on political grounds, it is recognised that issues about national priorities are unlikely to increase the overall funding for research. If certain subjects are categorised as priorities any resulting additional financial support can only be at the expense of all other subjects.

The result of the previous RAE has undoubtedly provided a boost to the status of research in the Institute. Research time is valued and protected. The proportion of research active staff continues to increase. Staff are active in all the research areas and bodies in Scotland and beyond. The Institute, therefore, looks forward to participating in the 1996 RAE. Its Strategic Plan has set demanding targets which it is hoped will be confirmed by its peers throughout the UK.

References

Wilson, J. and Perfect, H. (1985). 'Research', in Kirk, G. (Ed.) *Moray House and Professional Education 1835-1985,* Scottish Academic Press.

Moray House Institute of Education, 'Quality Assessment of Teaching and Learning: Self-Assessment', June 1994.

UFC (1992). 'Research Assessment Exercise 1992', Circular 5/92.

UFC (1992). 'Research Assessment Exercise 1992: The Outcome', Circular 26/92.

Joint Performance Indicators Working Group (July 1994), 'Management Statistics and Performance Indicators in Higher Education'.

10

Quality Assessment and Quality Audit

Gordon Kirk

The Commitment to Quality

Quality has become one of the watchwords of higher education in the 1990s. Partly in response to the need to be competitive, and partly to demonstrate professional and other forms of accountability, institutions have encumbered themselves with a welter of mechanisms for quality assurance, quality audit, quality control, quality enhancement and similar manifestations of the prevailing preoccupation. However, quality itself remains an elusive concept. For some, borrowing from industrial contexts, quality denotes fitness for purpose or compliance with specification: the value of an activity must be judged in relation to the ends that are sought. Since ends may be variable, quality is not an absolute but varies in relation to context. For others, however, particularly in academic contexts, quality denotes standards of achievement that are thought to be broadly comparable across institutions. Work of quality, in that sense, is work that reaches the highest levels of intellectual and professional accomplishment in relation to such values as truth, rationality, and respect for evidence.

However quality is defined, institutions are under pressure to profess their allegiance to it, to demonstrate that they can measure it, and to convince relevant stakeholders that they are committed to its enhancement. Indeed, the more an institution preoccupies itself with the quality of its work and the standards it achieves, the more difficult it is to establish a point at which the search for quality can be discontinued. It will always be appropriate to explore further ways of being more effective, of raising standards still higher, and of enhancing the work of an institution still further. Quality, in that sense, is not simply to be regarded as a finally established state of affairs: it is a process. The high-quality institution will be one in which there is a continuing commitment to establish still higher standards of quality.

That approach to quality implies that the responsibility for the maintenance of academic and professional standards rests with the whole academic community, including its students. Since questions of quality pervade the life of the institution, all must have a responsibility to contribute to the debate on quality enhancement, and all must come to realise that in their individual contributions to the life of an institution their primary concern is with the quality of that institution's work. Arguably, indeed, one of the distinguishing characteristics of a high-quality institution is that it fosters a vigorous culture of debate and discussion about how quality is to be maintained and enhanced. The whole mode of operation of an institution, then, should affirm the pervasiveness of the commitment to quality and should reinforce the principle that standards, above all else, are what ultimately matter.

Government Policy on Quality in Higher Education

The White Paper, *Higher Education: A New Framework,* 1991, set out the government's approach to quality in higher education. While the terms 'quality assurance' and 'quality control' enjoyed wide currency well before 1991 and, indeed, had been frequently used interchangeably, it was useful to have an official definition of the terms: 'quality assurance', according to the White Paper 'encompasses all the policies, systems and processes directed to ensuring maintenance and enhancement of the quality of educational provision'. On the other hand, 'quality control relates to the arrangements . . . which verify that teaching and assessment are carried out in a satisfactory manner'. That distinction reinforced the widely held view that, as in engineering contexts, quality control was concerned with the output of a process, whereas quality assurance was concerned with the prior steps necessary to ensure that the output was of an appropriate standard. The government's conceptual clarification, therefore, served to reinforce the familiar dictum that we should 'design quality in' (through quality assurance) as well as 'inspect faults out' (through quality control).

The most significant feature of the White Paper was the distinction it drew between quality audit and what was a new term in the lexicon of higher education, quality assessment. The first of these was seen as external scrutiny aimed at providing guarantees that institutions have suitable quality control mechanisms in place; quality assessment, on the other hand, was defined as the process of external evaluation of the actual provision of education.

The ensuing legislation of 1992 – the Further and Higher Education (Scotland) Act of 1992 and the corresponding English measure – made formal provision for quality assessment and quality audit. The Scottish Higher Education Funding Council (SHEFC) was empowered to secure that provision is made for assessing the quality of education in institutions through a Quality Assessment Committee. Quality audit, on the other hand, formally became a responsibility of all higher education institutions in the UK and became one of the functions of the Higher Education Quality Council, which is funded by subscription from institutions.

Quality Assessment

SHEFC has set out the aims of quality assessment in the following terms:

to provide a basis for advice to Council on the quality of educational provision in higher education institutions funded by SHEFC;

to provide reports which identify strengths and weaknesses, promote good practice and simulate improvement;

to monitor trends on the quality of provision relative to resources and the implementation of recommendations in earlier reports; and encourage progressive improvement by a programme of revisiting;

to provide a basis for advice to Council on the promotion and maintenance of quality through innovations and developments in curriculum, teaching and assessment;

to inform students and employers on the quality of provision thereby promoting competition and choice.

In order to discharge its responsibilities for quality assessment, SHEFC has developed a quality framework against which provision for teaching and learning in a cognate area is assessed by a panel of assessors who are trained for this purpose. The quality framework is as follows:

A   Aims and Curricula
B   Curriculum Design and Review
C   The Teaching and Learning Environment
D   Staff Resources
E   Learning Resources

F	Course Organisation
G	Teaching and Learning Practice
H	Student Support
J	Assessment and Monitoring
K	Students' Work
L	Output, Outcomes and Quality Control

When institutions are informed of the subject area that is to be assessed, they undertake a self-assessment for submission to SHEFC along with substantial documentation covering external examiners' reports, course evaluations, policy statements, and other evidence. Having analysed that documentation the panel visits the institution to meet groups of staff, to interview students, and to observe teaching and learning directly. Assessments of provision in an area is made against a four-point scale as follows:

> Excellent
> Highly Satisfactory
> Satisfactory
> Unsatisfactory

Since reports of quality assessments are made public there is every incentive for an institution to ensure that it achieves a high rating. Moreover, there are financial rewards, in the form of increases in funding places, for institutions which achieve a rating of excellent , and corresponding penalties for institutions which receive a rating of unsatisfactory in a particular area. Needless to say, one of the key purposes of this arrangement is to attract students to institutions judged to be providing courses of the highest quality.

Quality Audit

The objective of quality audit is to provide an effective mechanism for transmitting information and judgments about how higher education institutions, individually and collectively, fulfil their common responsibilities for maintaining and enhancing the quality of their educational provision and the standards of their awards . The audit procedure involves small groups of experienced auditors scrutinising institutions' procedures in the light of documentation and in the course of three-day visits to institutions. Audit teams normally operate through sampling the range of activities undertaken by an institution and by conducting audit trails , which pursue a line of questioning through a particular area of an institution's work. Again, audit reports are generated but, in this case, no final summary judgments is made of an institution. However, the opportunity is taken to identify features of an institution's work that are to be commended and to highlight those areas that may need further development. Since these reports are made public there is, again, a strong incentive for institutions to ensure that the outcome of the quality audit is positive.

While the quality audit process does not have the same kind of framework developed for quality assessment, there has been distributed a check-list for use by institutions in preparation for quality audit. That contains the following major headings:

The Institutional Context
Systems and Arrangements for Quality Assurance
The Design, Approval and Review of Programmes of Study
Teaching, Learning and Monitoring the Student Experience
Student Assessment and the Classification of Awards
Staff Appointment, Development, Promotion and Award
Content of Promotional Material in Relation to Academic Provision
Validation, Franchising and Other Forms of Collaborative
    Programme Provision

For each of these major headings a large number of criteria have been identified with the result that the quality audit of an institution is an extremely wide-ranging scrutiny of all aspects of its mode of operation.

Moray House and the Maintenance of Standards

There is no doubt that the advent of quality audit and quality assessment has provided a significant impetus to institutional discussion and the re-examination of standard practices. Institutions like Moray House, with long experience of working under the aegis of the Council for National Academic Awards, had become well accustomed to institutional visits and formal reporting on the standards of its work and how these standards are protected. How, then, does Moray House discharge these responsibilities?

There are two central features of the Moray House arrangements. The first of these is that all institutional procedures and the principles underpinning them are explicitly documented. Of course, the quality of the academic life sustained by an institution does not depend on adequate documentation alone. Nevertheless, good institutional practice depends on the adoption of shared views on procedure and the existence of explicit documentation on all aspects of quality assurance and quality control not only affirms an institution's educational philosophy but clarifies for all members of an academic community precisely how standards are to be upheld. At Moray House all of these principles are embodied in the Academic Standards Handbook.

The second feature of the Moray House approach is that there is strong external involvement in all aspects of its work – in the appointment of staff and students, in course design and planning, in placement supervision, in assessment, and in course evaluation. At every stage considerable care is taken to ensure that the work reflects good practice as it is judged by people of standing in other institutions of higher education and in the professions. Indeed, it is a feature of the institution's relationship with Heriot-Watt University that the body which formally makes recommendations to the Senate on academic matters has a majority of external specialists drawn from all parts of the United Kingdom.

The Quality of Staff

The quality of the work of an institution of higher education, its standing and reputation, and its impact on professional practice and scholarship, all depend, more than anything, on the quality of its staff. It has been assumed that the work of the Institute requires a preponderance of permanent full-time staff if a genuine academic community is to flourish, if continuity of course delivery is to be ensured, and if an authentic tradition of scholarly activity is to be maintained. At the same time, there is a need for alternative patterns of employment to enable the institution to respond appropriately to rapid fluctuations in demand, and to obtain regular infusions of new blood from the professions it serves. For these reasons the Institute has maintained a significant number of posts which are fixed-term, either on a full-time or part-time basis.

Moray House is primarily a teaching institution. While, of course, it seeks to ensure that teaching is underpinned by various forms of scholarly activity and is committed for academic and other reasons to the extension of its involvement in research and consultancy activities, it is the direct engagement with students that is the first and most important responsibility of staff, and it is that engagement which is the primary source of their satisfaction and achievement as well as their sense of professional identity: first and foremost they are teachers. Since, then, teaching constitutes the *métier* of the institution, and since the whole purpose of teaching is to foster learning, it is inevitable that the institution's perennial concern should be the quality of the learning it promotes. The institution is therefore preoccupied with enabling students to be enthusiastic about their studies, to foster their participation in the growth of their understanding, skills, and professional competence, and to support them in becoming autonomous learners in the sense that it becomes habitual for them to enquire, to question, to criticise and to evaluate, and to assume responsibility for the management of their own learning.

At the same time, it is recognised that effective teaching presupposes that staff are involved in research and other forms of scholarly activity of a kind that feeds into and sustains enterprising teaching. Other chapters of this volume describe the arrangements that are made to broaden and deepen the research base of the institution, and the range of consultancy and related activities in which staff engage to ensure that they remain at the forefront of professional practice. The Institute's recruitment policy seeks to ensure that staff are appointed who, as well as being accomplished professional practitioners, also have a record of successful engagement in research and development activities.

The Institute's policy maintains that the professional development of staff is essential in maintaining individual job satisfaction, enhancing the ability of staff to achieve the objectives of the Institute, and enabling the Institute to respond to rapid social, technological and educational change . Accordingly, the Institute has established practices to support and enhance the professional development of staff through a variety of means, including the up-grading of academic qualifications, through course and conference attendance, and through consultancy work at home and abroad. In addition, the equivalent of four weeks in the academic year are set aside for planned staff development activities of various kinds. In these periods, the professional development of staff has priority, even over the teaching of students.

Course Validation and Approval

No course is offered until it has undergone the Institute's course approval procedures. The purpose of these procedures is to ensure that, through a process of critical scrutiny by staff of the Institute and colleagues from the professions and other institutions, the course meets acceptable academic and professional standards, and the context of the course, including the human and physical resources necessary to sustain it, can guarantee a valid educational experience for course members. The validation process requires that careful scrutiny is undertaken of the rationale for the course; its aims and objectives; its structure, including placement and the sequence in which major units are phased; its teaching and learning strategies; its assessment; its admission arrangements; and the availability of the resources necessary to ensure that it can be effectively delivered. Not the least important of the matters for scrutiny is that the course planners require to demonstrate that the course will be taught by staff who have credible professional experience and who engage in research or other forms of scholarly work.

Annual Evaluation of Courses

Each year the course committee responsible for a programme is required to generate an evaluation report in order to enable the institution to judge whether or not it is proving successful and to identify difficulties that will require to be addressed. The annual evaluation report covers the following issues:

(a) cohort analysis: the number of applicants, the characteristics of entrants and student achievement;
(b) client satisfaction: the extent to which a course is valued by course members using the Institute's standard measure of client satisfaction;
(c) quality of teaching and learning;
(d) the appropriateness of course content;
(e) the appropriateness of the assessment of the course and of the ways in which it has been managed.

In conducting a formal evaluation of the course, the Institute draws on the experience of course tutors, the response of course members through the Institute's student module evaluation form, and the views of external examiners.

Course Reviews

Periodically, at least once every five years, every course is subjected to a major review. The purpose of such a review is to appraise the effectiveness of the course over a period, to assess the extent to which it has achieved the objectives set, and to determine whether or not these objectives take full account of educational, professional and other changes. The course review requires that documentation is generated which reflects discussion amongst those responsible for the course and their colleagues in the profession. In the light of the experience of running the course over a period, major changes are proposed if these are required. Again, the final judgment on the future development of the course is made by a group which includes a majority of external members.

External Examining

The external examining system is the key quality control mechanism in higher education. Through it institutions are able to determine whether or not, on the basis of the judgment of an external authority, their standards are in line with those of other institutions of higher education in the UK. External examiners are appointed by the Senate of the University and annually they are expected to determine that the assessment arrangements are fair and that standards are appropriate. Each year the Academic Standards Committee of the Institute considers all external examiners' reports and scrutinises the response made by course committees to these reports. In that way, the institution ensures that courses keep abreast of professional developments and that standards are maintained.

Internal Institutional Quality Audit

As a self-critical academic community, the Institute is committed to the periodic scrutiny of its own educational effectiveness and of the mechanisms and procedures it has established to maintain and enhance standards. To that end, the Institute has established an institutional research group, which also includes external representatives, to oversee a programme of research on the institution's own mode of operation following a programme determined by the Academic Board. The reports of this group constitute evidence which the Academic Board can use in its monitoring of the academic activities of the institution.

Issues

The introduction of quality assessment and quality audit has called for a significant investment of resources on the part of institutions and there is widespread concern about the amount of resources required by these activities. Some critics take the view that quality assurance and quality audit consume far too much valuable time and that the effect of addressing these major activities is that attention is deflected from the actual effective delivery of programmes. That criticism is reinforced by claims that there is a degree of duplication between quality audit and quality assessment. In a response to this claim, the Higher Education Quality Council has attempted to differentiate more clearly between audit and assessment. It has insisted that the scope of audit is considerably wider than that of assessment. It has also claimed that audit is concerned with systems and procedures, whereas assessment has actually been concerned with the nature of the educational provision that is made. Whether or not that differentiation is convincing, HEQC insists that there are benefits in having both systems in place. The 'warp and weft' approach is considered to be helpful and it is seen to be a strength of the system that different agencies in different ways can evaluate the work of institutions.

Notwithstanding these claims and counter-claims, there is no doubt that in the higher education community there is a strong belief that the two processes should be merged with both functions being performed by a single agency, preferably the Higher Education Quality Council. One reason for that claim is that the HEQC is owned by the institutions themselves; another reason for preferring that agency is that it does not make public summative judgments of quality on individual institutions. There is some evidence that the government is responding to the representations made by institutions. Gillian Shepherd, Secretary of State for Education, has recently indicated that the government is committed to examining the problem. In a recent address to the University Vice-Chancellors she stated:

> I recognise that the present separate assessment and audit programmes are seen as heavy-handed. I sympathise with those in universities who believe that these two programmes need to be brought together in one way or another in the next year or two . . . The timing of any change will need to be considered carefully. I hope those concerned will come together to develop a solution which I can support. I am asking the Funding Council to report to me by the Spring on a way forward, preferably a way forward which has been agreed with representative bodies in higher education.

One of the key areas of concern at present concerns the maintenance of standards at a time of resource constraint. All institutions of higher education are under severe financial pressure and have become used to operating in a climate in which 'efficiency gains' are required each year. The cumulative effect of this regime is that standards need to be maintained while resources are diminishing. It is widely held that it will be impossible for institutions to maintain quality in this context. Nevertheless, higher education institutions are caught in what might be called the quality trap . All of them are required to undertake self-assessments in each area of their academic work, and there is substantial pressure on institutions to claim in these self-assessments that their work is of 'excellent' standard. It is extremely difficult to square such claims with the view that resources are insufficient to enable quality to be maintained. Therefore, the continuation of a system of public and external scrutiny of institutions is a way of forcing them to take all possible steps to ensure that their work is of high quality, even although they may feel that the resources are not available to maintain standards. Time alone will tell whether the continuation of what might be termed 'academic blackmail' will serve to maintain standards or whether, because of a cumulative reduction in funding, standards really are threatened to the detriment of the higher education experience of students.

References

Moray House Institute of Education, *Academic Standards Handbook*, 1994.

Moray House Institute of Education, *Quality Assessment of Teaching and Learning in Initial Teacher Education: Self-Assessment*, 1994.

Scottish Higher Education Funding Council/Higher Education Quality Council, Joint Statement, *Quality Assessment and Quality Audit*, 1994.

Scottish Higher Education Funding Council, Circular 64/93, *Quality Assessment of Teaching and Learning*.

Higher Education Quality Council, *Notes for the Guidance of Auditors*, September 1993.

Higher Education Quality Council, *The Work of the Higher Education Quality Council*, July 1994.

Department for Education News: Statement by Gillian Shepherd, Minister for Education, 2 December 1994.

11

Equality and Education

Fernando Almeida Diniz

Introduction

This chapter is based on a belief that if inclusion in society is an objective, education and the law are two major means of attaining that objective. It will explore the impact of exclusionary forces on the life chances of particular groups in society, propose a reconceptualisation of the on-going debate and assess what progress the Institute has made in this area since the publication of *Moray House and Professional Education* in 1985 and its plans for the future.

Social Context for Change

The last 10 years have brought enormous global changes. A holocaust of poverty is affecting a fifth of the world's population and, nearer home, Europe has its own problems. The collapse of the Eastern Block, ethnic wars, refugee crises, chronic unemployment, and the rise of extreme right-wing parties are posing a real threat to social stability and have led a panel of experts assembled by Helmut Kohl and François Mitterand to recommend strongly to the European Union that the 1996 version of the Maastricht Treaty should empower the community's institutions to combat racism and xenophobia with as much vigour as they employ against sex discrimination. (CEC 1992; CE 1994).

Within Britain, it is impossible to ignore the legacy of political changes and economic policies of the 1980s, and, in particular, what seems to be a never-ending recession. There is unchallengeable evidence to demonstrate that the restructuring and re-segregation of work, the cycle of low pay, the abolition of wages councils, the operation of family and community pressures, domestic violence, employers' attitudes and political ideologies of motherhood including childcare, have had a disproportionate and devastating effect on the least powerful groups in society. Women, black/minority ethnic groups, disabled people, single parents, pensioners, homeless youth and whole communities have borne the full force of ideological policies in the 1980s. We now have a new category of what is termed an *underclass*, that is, the poor and dispossessed whose young children are in our schools, if they come at all. (Cohen 1992; Lister 1990; Robinson and Gregson 1992).

The lesson to be drawn from the above brief overview of global and national pressures is that all the world's people share equal responsibility for world peace, based on the principle of interdependence. There is an obligation on society as a whole to combat the exclusion of vulnerable groups by the operation of inclusive policies which aim to provide all people with access to the resources of society, irrespective of background and other distinguishing features.

Evidence of Exclusion

There is an abundance of documented evidence about the nature and extent of current exclusionary practices. The evidence summarized below is not confined to the debates within the education system, as this would give us only part of an entire picture. An acknowledgment that people's lives are multi-dimensional means that it is necessary to take a wider perspective by including employment, housing, health and social services. Similarly, whilst the research reviewed mainly stems from studies of gender, race and disability, it is accepted that there is an interplay of these factors and others (class, sexual orientation, political affiliation), which creates a multiplicity of discriminations. Where possible, research literature which comes from within Scotland will be reviewed, though its scarcity is a problem. (Brown *et al* 1994).

Employment and education are powerful indicators of inclusion in society: they bestow status and economic power, as well as being the means by which we are expected to make our contribution to society. How have women, black/minority ethnic groups and disabled people fared in the past decade?

Studies of employment provide some disconcerting findings.

- This is an area of rapid change with women forming a major part of the workforce; nevertheless they are under-represented in certain professions and in senior positions within the professions. Average earnings data show them to be substantially less paid than white men, particularly in Scotland, even when they have higher educational qualifications. There are few women in senior positions in the education service; the barriers frequently encountered are selection and recruitment processes, peer group pressures, the absence of childcare provision, experience of discrimination, and cosy traditional practices in management. Whereas we may be witnessing the increasing integration of women into such professions as teaching and social work, the status of these professions may be falling. High status professions (judges, consultants, professors) are still the preserve of white males. (Brown 1993; Breugel 1989, 1994; Cockburn 1991; Darling 1992; IRS 1992; Moss and Melhuish 1991; Rees 1992; Sokoloff 1992).

- Some labour market surveys have estimated unemployment rates for black/minority ethnic young women and men as high as 60%, with a disproportionate effect on black women. The annual report of the Commission for Racial Equality (CRE) showed widespread incidence of racial discrimination in the employment practices of British Rail, a large employment agency, and in a College of Further Education. The CRE's Code of Practice (Employment) issued in 1984 has been largely ignored. Black/minority ethnic women are likely to have immensely varying official participation rates in the labour market, with Afro-Carribeans having the highest rates and Pakistani and Bangladeshi women having the lowest rates. They are more likely than white women to work full-time, to be employed on a temporary and casual basis in sectors in which women predominate, to be undocumented as domestic workers and cleaners, to have no employee status and to be described as self-employed. Minority ethnic graduates encounter significant barriers in obtaining jobs and are generally less satisfied with the jobs they eventually obtain. They are less likely to be considered for promotion and to receive training (Bhavnani 1994; Breugel 1994; CRE 1989, 1990, 1992; Esmail and Everington 1993; Jenkins 1986; Jones 1993).

- Legislation intended to promote the employment of disabled people has been condemned as ineffective. School leavers continue to face overwhelming barriers of access, mobility, finance and attitudes in seeking employment, despite the introduction of new technologies. Brisenden (1989) notes perceptively that:

> . . . there is a major problem faced by the disabled school leaver, which is that nobody really believes that they can hold down a job. Everybody tries to dampen down their expectation, tries to make them feel grateful for what little is on offer. (p. 218).

The link between poverty and disability is most clearly argued in the OPCS (1988) study of disabled people in Britain by emphasizing the economic dimension of disablement. In common with black/minority ethnic groups and lone mothers, disabled people are disproportionately exposed to poverty resulting from poor housing, health and welfare reforms. The 1990 NHS and Community Care Act, designed to involve disabled people in the planning of services, will have profound implications for the future. (Amin and Oppenheim 1992; Brisenden 1989; Glendinning and Millar 1992; HMG Acts 1948, 1985, 1990; Lister 1992; Morris 1988).

Studies of Education and Training provide findings which give similar cause for concern.

- Gender inequality is still a feature of the education system. Rarely is it recognised that the majority of pupils referred to special education are boys. There is rising concern that, throughout the education system, boys are failing to achieve. Girls continue to experience institutionalised sexism as part of their daily lives. The failure of teachers to take girls' contribution seriously and the concessions made by careers services to occupational segregation in the labour market are still in evidence. The fact that girls out-perform boys in academic achievement, and that there are more women studying on engineering and science courses in Scotland, may be taken to mean that all is well. It may also explain why gender inequality has received little attention here. Fewell and Paterson have suggested that the reality of institutionalised sexism has been concealed by a mythology of the excellence and egalitarianism of Scottish education, closely tied to Scottish national identity. (Bamber 1988; Cooper *et al* 1991; Fewell and Paterson 1990; Riddell 1992; Weiner 1985).
- Racism in education has been highlighted in studies across Europe and officially recognised in government reports. There is clear evidence of racial harassment, name-calling and violence in schools. Recent initiatives on bullying appear to give little attention to this trend. Minority ethnic pupils are over-represented in segregated special education because their bi-cultural and bilingual status is frequently ignored. Their parents are rarely consulted in a meaningful way and more recently black boys and girls are being excluded from education altogether. In Scotland, while the research community has yet to address this area of policy, the same issues are beginning to surface. (Bourne *et al* 1994;

Brah and Minhas 1992; Curnyn *et al* 1990; Gillborn 1992; MacDonald Inquiry 1990; OECD 1987; Shah 1992).

- The special education system continues to be a source of controversy and is likely to remain so. After decades of attempts at integration, there is evidence that segregation is on the increase. This is occurring, particularly in urban areas across Europe, despite a torrent of calls from eminent bodies (e.g. UNESCO) for the inclusion of disabled pupils in mainstream education. Disabled people and their organisations are increasingly advocating the dismantling of the segregated sector whilst some parents seem to be moving the other way by demanding specialised placements. (Allan *et al* 1991; Barton 1988; Brown 1994; Garner 1993; Norwich 1990; Oliver 1989; UN 1993; UNESCO/Govt. of Spain 1994).

- Higher education has been particularly slow to tap the potential that exists in large sectors of society. There are differential acceptance rates to universities for black and white, disabled and able-bodied, male and female students. For example, acceptance criteria themselves have been found to be discriminatory. In one study, analysis of the 1990 and 1991 data showed that Bangladeshis, Pakistanis, Afro-Carribeans and Black-Others were under-represented in acceptances. A study conducted a year later concluded that, even after significant academic and social factors are taken into account, some form of ethnic differences in the rates of admission to universities and polytechnics remained unexplained, with Pakistanis and Afro-Carribeans experiencing the greatest barriers. Colleges and universities are equally unwelcoming institutions as employers of ethnic minorities and women. A further relevant study examined equity and management in further and higher education institutions, in particular the experience of women and minority ethnic managers. Among the obstacles identified were racism, sexism, harassment, exploitation, ageism, invisibility and patronising attitudes. (Modood and Shiner 1994; Powney and Weiner 1991; Taylor 1993).

Have equal opportunities policies made a difference? Most education authorities have over the last decade introduced policies which schools and colleges are meant to implement, though few have been evaluated to detect qualitative change. However, even where organisations had such policies, only a few reported an increase in the proportion of black/minority ethnic or disabled people employed; they seem to be insufficiently aware of their legal duties and of the Codes of Practice on disability, employment practice and racial equality. Companies may also be operating discriminatory practices in the recession, viewing equal opportunities policies as costly. Two reports by the CRE contain recommendations directed towards institutes of higher education. They call for clear written policy statements which cover admissions, the educational experiences of students and outcomes, including employment, thorough implementation across all departments, monitoring and student support services. Tutors themselves are expected to demonstrate commitment to these policies (Brennan and McGeevor 1990; CRE 1989; Jenkins and Solomos 1989). Introducing one of the CRE reports, Day, the Chief Executive of the CRE, says:

> *What is apparent is that, compared with schools, universities and polytechnics have been relatively untouched by the debate on racial equality in education and have not, on the whole, seen the need to develop specific policies in this area. It may be that these institutions have seen themselves as incapable of discrimination or unequal treatment, and thus absolved from discussions of inequality in access to educational opportunity.* (CRE 1989).

Does research on equality in Scotland point to similar conclusions? A recent report by the Equal Opportunities Commission has concluded that research on women in Scotland is of limited scope and depth: it has been descriptive, failing to produce explanations and develop theoretical frameworks, is poorly resourced, and does not reach practitioners (Brown et al 1994). Research in Scotland has also remained colour-blind: the first survey of black/minority people made the claim that *those better qualified than us . . . will be able to use our findings to draw conclusions and make recommendations. One of the results of taking this approach is that we do not discuss racial discrimination.* (Smith, 1991 p.9). It is hoped that policy-makers, research bodies and academics will take note of the need for research in equal opportunities.

Whereas research which would lead to greater understanding of the multiple nature of discrimination is clearly needed, it should also be recognised that this task faces a number of obstacles. These include assumptions which preclude its necessity, and a tendency to concentrate on single categories without a recognition of diversity within and across categories. There are, in addition, theoretical questions about the sort of knowledge that is required: is the paradigm one of equal opportunity or one predicated on equity, rights, injustice and oppression? Conducting research of this kind also raises particular methodological challenges: for example, who sets the research agenda? Are there ethical problems involved in white researchers studying black experience? Access to research may not simply relate to the agenda but also to the research function itself. Adopting an emancipatory approach may help in avoiding the reproduction of unequal power relationships within the research context and may also ensure that the results have a positive impact on the life-chances of marginalised groups. (Diniz, 1995).

What conclusion might be drawn from the above analysis in order to inform future policy change? The growth of knowledge about the nature of human society has helped ordinary people to become aware of forms of discrimination which affect their lives and to demand better justice. There is overwhelming evidence of the existence and persisting effects of exclusionary forces in all sectors of social life. Discrimination is not even-handed in its impact on different groups but is damaging for all and must be tackled by society as a whole.

New Paradigm: Equity and Rights?

What do we know about the concept of *discrimination* itself? The Convention of the International Labour Office was possibly the first to use the term when it defined discrimination as any distinction, exclusion or preference made on the basis of race, colour, sex, religion, political opinion, national extraction or social origin. This definition maintained that differential treatment of persons supposed to belong to a particular group was unlawful. It is important to note that not all discriminatory practice need be unlawful: free travel passes for senior citizens is an example of lawful discrimination, although whether such a practice is morally justified is open to dispute. Another important distinction which still causes confusion is that between discrimination as a form of behaviour (involving power relations) and prejudice as a personal attitude. The major sources of discrimination are now acknowledged to stem from institutional and structural barriers, not necessarily from prejudice, and can take the form of direct and indirect discrimination. Social scientists have taken an increasing interest in the concept; economists are able to explain the differences between male and female participation in employment; sociologists have tackled issues of how discriminatory practices come to characterise particular kinds of social structure (for example, the existence of a segregated school system); and psychologists can illuminate why some groups are more likely to behave in discriminatory ways than others. Thus, a great deal is known about the theoretical basis of discrimination. Despite these advances, Banton (1994) has observed that the concept itself is still in the course of development and 'its implications have not been fully worked out and even its basic character is not always understood'. This conclusion may explain why discussions about discrimination are so often taken as accusations, which in turn provoke a defensiveness likely to interfere with an examination of the facts.

Analyses conducted by social scientists have led to an acknowledgment that race, gender and disability are economically, politically, ideologically and socially constructed: they are context-specific, changing phenomena and represent the immense diversity, heterogeneity and differentiation of the historical and cultural experiences of people (New Community 1993). It is perhaps for this reason that theoretical explanations based on single category discrimination have failed to make an impact on practice and suggest why there is a need for more sophisticated conceptual frameworks which express the commonality of human experience, whilst respecting the uniqueness of particular groups within society. Such a shift of paradigm, away from categories, needs, deficits and theories of assimilation, normalisation and integration, towards an explicit acceptance of *Diversity* and the inclusion of all, based on the principle of *Equity and Rights*, may be more fruitful.

The term *equity* appeared in the educational literature at a time when conservative politicians began to attack the notion of *equality*, associating it with liberal egalitarianism, progressive methods and left-wing councils. There have also been criticisms of the ambiguous definitions of equality in the anti-discrimination legislation and in equal opportunities policy documents (Diniz 1992). In addition, account needs to be taken of the negative reaction by many to the use of the terms anti-sexism, anti-racism, anti-discrimination (Davies 1990). The merit of adopting an equity and rights perspective is that it represents the ideal of fairness and social justice linked to the law.

The term *rights* has become part of everyday vocabulary in the quest for social justice. This understanding is based on a range of declarations of human rights by the United Nations, the European Court and in the written constitutions of national states. As we approach the twenty-first century, there is increasing pressure on governments to ensure human rights, citizenship and democracy. For example, disabled people in Britain have argued for their de-segregation in society through the guarantee of their human rights in legislation similar to the Disabilities Act of 1990 in the USA. The UK has enacted anti-discrimination legislation in a number of aspects of social policy (for example, Sex Discrimination Act 1975, 1986; Disabled Persons Act 1944, 1958, 1986; Race Relations Act 1976; Children Act 1989). Given that our government has also ratified various international conventions, such as those of the United Nations, the

International Labour Organisation, and the European Court of Human Rights, there is no shortage of legal instruments to combat discriminatory practice. The weakness has resided in the implementation and monitoring of codes of practice and other guidance governing legislation (Banton 1994; Parekh 1991; SEMRU 1993).

Citizenship and *Democracy* are now fashionable topics on the agendas of politicians. The Conservative government's moral crusade for active citizenship and the opposition's demands for the European Convention on Human Rights to be incorporated in British Law are examples of the current debate. The issue of citizenship rights has also begun to be addressed by particular groups: Lister (1990) discussed the rights of women, Smith (1989) discussed race, and Driedger (1989) has dubbed the struggles of disabled people as the last civil rights movement. In a discussion of the relationship between equality and democracy, Arblaster (1993) points to a tension between the continued existence of economic and social inequalities and the democratic principle of political equality, which ought to mean not merely equality in the voting booth but also equality of access to the political decision-makers, and equal opportunities to influence the policies and direction taken by society as a whole.

Adopting an *Equity and Rights* paradigm poses challenges for practitioners. It demands a critical understanding of concepts of rights, citizenship, and democracy, a thorough knowledge of the increasing array of anti-discriminatory legislation informing global politics, and the commitment to ensure that education is directed to the development of respect for human rights and fundamental freedoms. (UN Rights of the Child, 1989 Art 29).

Institutional Practice in Moray House

In *Moray House and Professional Education* (1985), Landon stated 'Although a start has been made . . . the College is a long way from permeating all its courses with multi-cultural and anti-racist principles'. What progress has been made and what needs to be done in the sphere of equality of opportunity? This section considers relevant aspects of institutional change, illustrating how policy and practice have developed in three main areas: Moray House Equal Opportunity Policy; curriculum development for professional education, and innovation and research.

Equal Opportunity Policy

Moray House adopted its current policy on Equality of Opportunity (EO) in 1990 after three years of consultation and development. Since then, the focus has broadened to encompass the full range of equity and rights issues discussed above. The Institute has taken account of and been involved in similar developments in public sector organisations, mainly the Scottish Office Education Department, the regional authorities and bodies concerned with the oversight of professional education and training, such as the General Teaching Council (GTC), the Central Council for the Education and Training of Social Workers (CCETSW) and Community Education, Validation and Endorsement (CeVe).

Moray House staff have acted as consultants to policy-making bodies and as in-service trainers across Scotland and in Europe. This broad range of activity and experience has been vital in promoting equality of opportunity and has required the Institute to address its own policies and procedures to ensure that they reflect the needs of a changing and pluralist society.

The Academic Board has conducted an audit of practice and developed an implementation strategy with specific targets dealing with academic leadership, marketing, recruitment, curriculum development and management training and responsibility. Management and academic responsibility has now been established. The senior assistant principal has been allocated overall institutional responsibility for the policy and a senior lecturer in equity and rights in education has been appointed to provide academic leadership of the field across the Institute in teaching, research and consultancy activities.

Finally, in relation to staff recruitment, a number of steps have been taken to ensure that recruitment and selection of staff and students comply with equal opportunities good practice: job descriptions and person specifications are produced for all posts; application forms have been amended in line with good EO practice; training in fair interviewing for all those involved in staff and student selection has taken place; selection panels are balanced in terms of ethnicity and gender; monitoring data is being collected; and procedures for publishing and acting upon the results of that monitoring are being developed. Though these positive steps are being taken, the implementation strategy is relatively recent and the next priority is to ensure that it is monitored and reviewed on a regular basis to maintain momentum.

Professional Education: Equal Opportunities Module in Undergraduate Courses

A significant change has taken place in teaching. In 1993, the re-validation of Institute courses offered the opportunity to include EO as a compulsory element in undergraduate programmes. The chosen approach was a mixture of permeation and discrete modular provision. While course leaders and tutors throughout the Institute were asked to address EO issues, the Department of Professional Development and Community Education designed and now delivers a half module entitled *Equal Opportunities and Anti-Discriminatory Practice*. The core module is contextualised for each of the programmes in primary education, in physical education, in technology, in community education, and in social work. The course covers theoretical perspectives, analyses of evidence of discrimination, and identifies some key implications for professional action. The module has been revised to minimise the didactic elements and to maximise interactive opportunities. Though every attempt is made to use the most up-to-date and relevant information, the lack of Scottish research on equality issues is a major problem. Nevertheless, Moray House can commend itself for adopting the module as a feature of its curriculum and institutional policy.

Professional Education: Equal Opportunities in the Modular Masters Scheme

Several specialist Masters degree programmes, underpinned by equality perspectives, have been developed over the past five years. In the major area of special educational needs, there is a range of awards and specialisms in disability and learning difficulties. Clusters of modules specifically concerned with equality issues have been developed and will be available to students either as awards in equality opportunities or as part of other awards. As part of the Institute's strategy for implementing its equal opportunity policy, it is proposed for the future that all students on Masters degree programmes will be required to follow a module on anti-discriminatory practice as is the case in undergraduate programmes.

Centres for Innovation and Research

Moray House has been particularly successful in securing external funding and since 1991 has established a number of national centres, dedicated to innovation in specific areas of equality practice. These all undertake research, offer consultancy, and provide training and support to professionals across Scotland. All the Centres have gained international recognition.

- **The Scottish Sensory Centre** (SSC) was created by amalgamating The Scottish Centre for the Education of the Deaf and the Visual Impairment Centre, both based in Moray House. SSC is funded by SOED to promote and support new developments and effective practice in the education of children and young people with sensory impairment from birth to 19 years. The central feature of its work is to enable young people to gain full access to education by overcoming barriers to learning which may be caused by their sensory loss or by lack of knowledge or access to resources on the part of those responsible for their education. SSC staff help in the struggle for equality of access by various means – by providing information services through databases, by liaison with education authorities, voluntary and statutory organisations, by the development of curricular and assessment support materials, by short courses on topics identified by clients and Centre staff, and by a lending library service of books, videos and other resources. SSC has organised British Sign Language classes for students and for interested staff in the Institute and at Heriot-Watt University. The Centre has also advised staff and students with sensory impairment. From 1994, the co-ordinator of SSC now has an official role, funded by the Scottish Higher Education Funding Council, to advise and support staff and students with sensory impairment.

- **The Centre for Specific Learning Difficulties/Dyslexia** was established through funding by the Scottish Dyslexia Trust. It has also recently been supported by SOED. The main purpose of the Centre is to influence professional practice throughout Scotland by providing high-level training courses and conferences, and by publication. It also provides support for dyslexic learners and their families. During 1995, it will be engaged in developing a national network of resource centres, in collaboration with other teacher education institutions in Scotland.

- **The Scottish Traveller Education Project** (STEP) is funded by SOED and aims to promote the education of travellers. This group has been identified by the European Commission as one of the most marginalized because the education system has failed to take account of their lifestyle and cultural traditions. STEP is engaged in European-wide initiatives to enhance professional practice and make schools more inclusive. It has been highly praised for the distance-learning material which was produced at Moray House and has now been adopted in other EU states. STEP maintains effective links with traveller communities.

- **The Centre for Education for Racial Equality in Scotland** (CERES) is funded by SOED. The work of CERES is doubled-edged. It seeks to improve the quality of provision in terms of access and experience for all ethnic groups, as well as working towards the elimination of racism and racial discrimination in educational institutions throughout Scotland. It has targeted pump-priming work within local authorities with small black/minority ethnic populations and networked with national bodies in the area of curriculum design and implementation through the SCCC, GTC, and SOED. CERES continues to play a crucial role in galvanising the participation of minority ethnic communities on all levels, since they are under-represented in national bodies, school boards and parent organisations.

- **Community languages** initiatives which support linguistic minorities within Scotland are few in number, apart from the teaching of Gaelic. The Nuffield Interpreters Project and EU Intercultural Project are specifically designed to enhance the status and use of minority community languages. The Nuffield project trains public service interpreters and the Intercultural Project is specifically aimed at supporting bilingual learners in isolated areas throughout the UK. Moray House is recognised as a centre of excellence in this field.

- **The Centre for Counselling Education** is the most recent project and is designed to promote the theory and practice of this developing field. The pressures faced by individuals in society are illustrated by some of the themes of the courses provided by the Centre: bereavement, couple relationships, addiction, HIV/AIDS, cross-cultural counselling, sexual abuse and post-traumatic stress. The training of professional counsellors is a major priority as is the provision of a counselling service.

Research on Equality Issues in Scotland

As was pointed out earlier, there is a serious shortage of research on equality issues in Scotland. These centres not only undertake research but engage in development work which is intended to impact directly on professional practice. In addition, Moray House has participated in discussions with the Equal Opportunities Commission, the Commission for Racial Equality and other relevant bodies to devise a strategy for more effective action. CERES has recently established the *Education for Racial Equality Research Network* to spearhead research in this sphere. It will co-operate with other Scottish networks, for example, the *Gender in Education Network*.

Conclusion

At the start of this chapter, reference was made to the existence of major pressures facing the world community and the need for all of us to act to address these issues. Within the context of Scotland there is evidence of continuing discriminatory practice in all aspects of social life. That should serve as a reminder to us to give thought to the legacy we shall leave to future generations. It should also serve as a stimulus to further effort. Moray House intends to play a vigorous part in that challenging work.

Note: I wish to thank my colleagues Rowena Arshad, Alan Bell, Marianna Buultjens, Elizabeth Jordan, Colin Kirkwood, John Landon and Gavin Reid for their assistance in writing this chapter.

References

Allan, J., Brown, S. and Munn, P. (1991). *Off the Record: mainstream provision for pupils with non-recorded learning difficulties in primary and secondary schools,* Edinburgh, SCRE.

Amin, K. and Oppenheim, C. (1992) *Poverty in Black and White,* Child Poverty Action Group.

Arblaster, A. (1993). *Democracy,* Open University Press.

Bamford, C. (1988). *Gender in Education in Scotland: a review of research,* Edinburgh, SIACE.

Banton, M., (1994). *Discrimination,* OU Press.

Barton (1988) *The Politics of Special Educational Needs,* Falmer.

Bhavnani, R. (1994). *Black women in the labour market: a research review* ,EOC.

Bourne, J., Bridges, L. and Searle, C. (1994). *Outcast England: How schools exclude black children,* Institute of Race Relations.

Brah, A. and Minhas, R. (1992). Structural racism or cultural difference: schooling for Asian girls in Weiner G. (Ed.) *Just a Bunch of Girls,* OU Press.

Brennan, J. and McGeevor, P. (1990). *Ethnic minorities and the graduate market,* CRE.

Breugel, I. (1989). Sex and Race in the labour market, *Feminist Review* 32.

Breugel, I, (1994). Labour market prospects for women from ethnic minorities in Lindley, R. (Ed.) *Labour market structures and prospects for women,* EOC Research Series.

Brisenden, S. (1989). Young, gifted and black: entering the employment market, *Disability, Handicap and Society* 4, 217-220.

Brown, A., Breithenbach, E. and Myers, F. (1994). *Equality Issues in Scotland: a research review,* EOC.

Brown, S. (1993). Research on Gender in Education: monitoring bleakness or instigating change? *Scottish Affairs* 5, 107-17.

Brown, S. (1994). Multiple policy innovations: in impact on special educational needs provision, *British Journal of Special Education* 21 3, 97-100.

Cockburn, C. (1991). *In the way of women: men's resistance to sex equality in organisations,* Macmillan.

Cohen, R. (1992). *Hardship Britain: being poor in the 1990s,* Child Poverty Action Group.

Commission for Racial Equality (CRE) (1984). *Code of Practice: for elimination of racial discrimination and the promotion of equality of opportunity in employment,* CRE.

Commission for Racial Equality (CRE) (1989). *Are Employers Complying? a research reprint* ,CRE.

Commission for Racial Equality (CRE) (1989). *Words or Deeds? Review of Equal Opportunity Policies in Higher Education,* CRE.

Commission for Racial Equality (CRE) (1992). *Annual Report 1991*, CRE.

Commission of the European Communities (1992). *Legal Instruments to combat racism and xenophobia,* Luxembourg.

Cooper, P., Upton, G. and Smith, C. (1991). Ethnic minority and gender distribution among staff and pupils in facilities for pupils with emotional and behavioural difficulties in England and Wales, *British Journal of Sociology of Education* 12, 1, 77-94.

Council of Europe (CE) (1994). Update on final report: *Community and ethnic relations in Europe,* published in 1992.

Curnyn, J., Wallace, I., Kistan, S. and McLaren, M. (1990). Special educational need and ethnic minority pupils *Professional Development Initiatives 1989-90,* SOED/ Regional Psychological Services.

Darling, J. (1992). The best man for the job: women teachers, promotion and the Strathclyde research, *Scottish Educational Review.*

Davies, L. (1990). *Equity and Efficiency,* Falmer.

Diniz, F. A. (1992). *Introduction to 5-14 developments and the elimination of racial discrimination within Scottish education?* Conference report: CERES, Edinburgh.

Diniz, F. A. (1995). *Researching racial equality issues in Scottish education,* Occasional Paper 1: Centre for Education for Racial Equality in Scotland, Edinburgh.

Dreidger, D. (1989). *The last civil rights movement* ,Disabled People's International, London.

Esmail, A. and Everington, S. (1993). Racial discrimination against doctors from ethnic minorities, *British Medical Journal 36,* March.

Fewell, J. and Paterson, F. (1990). *Girls in their prime: Scottish education re-visited,* Scottish Academic Press.

Garner, P. (1993). Exclusions: the challenge to schools, *Support for Learning 8,* 99-103.

Gillborn, D. (1992). Racism and education: issues for research and practice in Brown, S. and Riddell, S. (Eds.) *Class, Race and Gender in Schools,* Edinburgh, SCRE/EIS.

Glendinning, C. and Millar, J. (1992). *Women and poverty in Britain, the 1990s,* Harvester Wheatsheaf.

HMG (UK) Acts: Disbled Persons (Employment) (1948); Companies Act (1985); Sex Discrimination (1975/1986); Race Relations (1976); Children's Act (1989).

Industrial Relations Services (IRS) (1992). *Pay and gender in Britain 2,* IRS.

International Labour Organisation (ILO) (1958). Convention III, Discrimination (Employment and Occupation).

Jenkins, P. and Solomos, J. (1989). *Racism and equal opportunities policies in the 1980s,* Cambridge University Press.

Jenkins, R. (1986). *Racism and recruitment: managers, organisations and equal opportunity in the labour market,* Cambridge University Press.

Jones, T. (1993). *Britain's Ethnic Minorities,* Policy Studies Institute.

Kirk, G. (1985). *Moray House and Professional Education 1835-1985,* Scottish Academic Press.

Lister, R. (1990). *The Exclusive Society: citizenship and the poor,* Child Poverty Action Group.

Lister, R. (1992). *Women's Economic Dependence and Social Security,* Equal Opportunity Commission.

Macdonald Inquiry (1990). *Murder in the playground,* Longsight Press.

Modood, T. and Shiner, M. (1994) *Ethnic minorities in higher education. Why are there differential rates of entry?* Policy Studies Institute/UCAS.

Morris, J. (1988). *Freedom to lose: housing policy and people with disabilities,* Shelter, London.

Moss, P. and Melhuish, E. (1991). *Current issues in day care for young children*, HMSO.

New Community (1993). *Race, ethnicity and gender relations. New Community*, Vol. *19*, April.

Norwich, B. (1990). *Reappraising Special Needs Education*, Cassell.

OECD (1987). *Immigrant children at school*. Paris: CERI.

Oliver, M. (1989). Conductive education: if it wasn't so sad it would be funny *Disability, Handicap, Society 4*, 197-200.

OPCS (1988). *Disability in Britain*, London.

Parekh, B. (1991). Law torn. *New Statesmen and Society* .14 June, 1991.

Powney, J. and Weiner, G. (1991). *Outside the norm: equity and management in educational institutions*, Dept. of Education, South Bank University.

Rees, T. (1992). *Women and the labour market*, Routledge.

Riddell, S. (1992). Gender and education: progressive and conservative forces in the balance in Brown, S. and Riddell, S. (Eds.) *Class, Race and Gender in Schools*, Edinburgh, SCRE/EIS.

Robinson, F. and Gregson, N. (1992). The underclass, *Critical Social Policy 34*, Summer.

Scottish Ethnic Minorities Research Unit (SEMRU) (1993). *Anti-discrimination Law Summary of findings and recommendations*, Edinburgh College of Art.

Shah, R. (1992). *The Silent Minority: children with disabilities in Asian families*, National Children's Bureau.

Smith (1989). *The politics of race and residence*, Polity Press, Cambridge.

Smith, P. (1991). *Ethnic minorities in Scotland*, Scottish Office.

Sokoloff, N. (1992). *Black women and white women in the profession*, Routledge.

Taylor, P. (1993). Minority ethnic groups and gender in access to higher education, *New Community 19*.

UN (1989). *Convention on the Rights of the Child*, New York: UN.

UN (1993). *Standard rules on the equalization of opportunities for persons with disabilities*, New York: UN.

UNESCO/Govt. of Spain (1994). *Draft framework for action on Special Needs education*, Salamanca declaration, Paris: UNESCO.

Weiner, G. (1985). *Just a bunch of girls*, Open University Press.

12

Consultancy and Professional Development

James O'Brien

A Context of Innovation and Development

In the last 10 years the range of fundamental innovation at system level suggests that Scottish schools have experienced change on an unprecedented scale, confirming the views expressed in the earlier Moray House volume and by other commentators (Perfect, 1985; Brown and Munn, 1985).

National developments in schooling have dominated the past decade. These have been concerned with the curriculum in general, and have involved the continued consolidation of secondary educational reforms deriving from the introduction of Standard Grade, the seepage of National Certificate modules into S3/S4, and the introduction of Revised Higher. More recently, the 'Higher Still' proposals (SOED, 1994) indicate another major development programme which will include *inter alia* reviewing existing good practice, publishing curricular guidelines, overseeing transitional arrangements, and developing the new framework of courses and awards in an integrated scheme. To achieve such an ambitious programme at a time when many teachers are claiming 'innovation fatigue' and expressing concerns about overall workload will require a substantial amount of staff development to promote and prepare for the unified curriculum and assessment system envisaged for post-Standard Grade certification in schools and further education colleges.

Additionally, since 1984, the Technical and Vocational Education Initiative (TVEI) has been instrumental in promoting enhanced teaching and learning approaches, the use of new technologies, vocational education, guidance and a concern for equal opportunities in a range of secondary schools throughout the country (SED, 1989). In the early years of secondary schools (Goulder, Simpson *et al*, 1994) and in the primary sector, the 5-14 Development Programme (Roger and Hartley, 1990; Harlen and Malcolm 1994) now promotes a range of activity, albeit with the growing acceptance that a longer more phased approach to change is necessary. Proposals and legislation relating to devolved school management (SOED, 1992; Hartley, 1994) and the 'governance' of schools (School Boards Act, 1988; Macbeth, 1990) have also been supported by national and local in-service opportunities and staff development, including comprehensive national provision in support of management training for head teachers (Alexander, Havard *et al*, 1992).

While there have been many local and regional initiatives on such pressing concerns as the introduction of information technology and the development of equal opportunities policies, most local developments have reflected national reforms. School development planning (Hargreaves and Hopkins, 1991), and staff development and appraisal reflect this trend. All of these developments have contributed to an unprecedented 'agenda for change', and what has been described by commentators as 'policy hysteria' (Stronach and Morris, 1994).

Such a series of innovations and major policy initiatives suggests at least an unease at government level about the 'results' of schooling. The response to the low achievement of schools was thought to lie in managing schools and the curriculum more *effectively*. The critique of schooling and the searching for remedies through moves to efficiency have been a UK phenomenon and have certainly not been restricted to Scotland. Indeed, it has been strongly suggested that the changes here have been part of a process of 'anglicization' of Scottish education, although in a study of the early part of the 5-14 Development Programme this view is rejected (Goulder, Simpson *et al*, 1994). Nevertheless, it would be fair to state that reforms have emerged because pupil attainments have been viewed as inadequate and the belief that standards must be raised dominates innovation (Brown, 1992). The resulting changes have confirmed a tendency towards greater centralisation influenced by curricular guidelines and national testing, while conversely local participation in school management with an enhanced role for parents reflects an increasing policy reliance on 'market forces' (Gilbert, 1990) and a belief that consumerism can effect change in schools.

The innovations in schools of the last decade therefore have been increasingly fuelled by an elixir distilled from the school of 'management and effectiveness', with reform and renewal in education being served also by an emphasis on 'direct accountability between consumer and producer' (Ransom, 1990) and 'quasi-market ideology' (Brown, 1994). In-service support, professional development and consultancy have, in turn, not been neglected by the demands of such 'market forces'. The decade has been characterised by a model of INSET which is driven by central government through the publication of annual national priorities and the overt resourcing and sponsorship of national initiatives such as the curriculum reforms already referred to, as well as management reforms such as the Staff Development and Appraisal initiative (Kirk and Cameron-Jones, 1994). While the national determination of in-service priorities will undoubtedly continue, there is a trend towards more localised decision-making in which provision will be determined by schools as purchasers of provision to meet their needs.

Community Education and Social Work, those other major areas of provision in which the Institute is involved, have not escaped change and development. There has been an increasing recognition of the need for high quality post-qualification staff development for professionals in these fields, and relevant developments are described in Chapters 5 and 6 of this volume.

National Changes in the Funding and Provision of In-Service

In 1985, the college of education sector received a generous staffing allowance to provide support for in-service and staff development (Kirk, 1988). Since that time the funding position for in-service, consultancy and professional development has been radically altered. Five years ago, 54.5 full-time equivalent staff at Moray House were funded for in-service education purposes. Today, less than half that number is similarly engaged, but without the perceived security of government grant-in-aid funding their efforts. During the same period, the locus of INSET has become increasingly the school, and as a result college-based in-service and longer courses have declined.

The government-inspired change to the funding of teachers' professional development has resulted in the creation of a market: Moray House, like any other higher education institution, now pays for staffing and resources through 'income-generating activities', when no grant-in-aid funding is available. The Institute now competes against other providers, including local authority agencies and personnel, by responding to 'calls for tender' and bidding for specific contracts. How has this market economy emerged?

In England and Wales in the mid-80s it was considered that the resources for teacher education were not used to best advantage. Inevitably, the approaches borrowed or adapted from those common south of the border began to influence the Scottish pattern of provision. TVEI-related in-service training (TRIST) applicable to those Scottish authorities that had taken up the overall initiative, paved the way between

1985 and 1987. Education authorities were free to bid for allocations of grant for training purposes and on occasion to go beyond traditional providers. Through this initiative the era of the hotel-based course and the network of local authority and school-based co-ordinators of in-service and staff development began. However, TRIST also introduced important ideas of training specification and methods of provision, as well as monitoring and evaluation to ensure quality and subsequent action. For teacher participants such 'business-like' courses, with associated trappings, appeared to be an approach in keeping with their standing as professionals and was far removed from the fare usually available in teacher centres or college refectories. There was also a concern for 'value for money' associated with training and for change to be effected in schools as a result of training intervention. Schools and their personnel were to be improved in this way.

TRIST was quickly followed in England by an approach that applied to all local authority in-service training and was known as Grant Related In-service Training (GRIST). This approach quickly became more commonly known as the Local Education Authority Training Grants Scheme (LEATGS). Associated with this scheme was the annual publication of national training priorities for school teachers. These developments had several repercussions: from a training and development standpoint, the expectations of teachers about the quality of provision were raised; local authorities drifted towards funding their own in-service and staff development services; and a cycle of planning, implementation, evaluation and review was beginning to emerge.

Inevitably, the higher education system had to adjust its provision as the emphasis shifted from the secondment of teachers released for full-time courses. The increased demand for clearly focused short courses and in-school development accelerated moves towards modularisation of courses and masters awards schemes that were based on credit accumulation and transfer (CATS), and John Landon analyses the changes in this field and the Moray House response in Chapter 7 of this volume. It has been argued by Hargreaves (1994) that the switch from traditional INSET that was characterised by lengthy courses or *ad hoc* provision to staff development and subsequently to the concept of professional development is a direct result of education reforms and devolution of budgets. Hargreaves maintains that professional development is the result of accepting that teachers have life-long professional needs; as a result, there needs to be regular assessment of individual teachers in order to identify needs which have then to be taken into account along with needs which are identified from school review and development planning. Planning for development with appropriate opportunities designed increasingly for a group or team rather than individuals, with a growing interest in action research techniques, including the use of external consultants, has emerged as a dominant approach to meeting individual needs within the framework of agreed school policies (Newton and Tarrant, 1992). To an extent, this approach is being driven by teachers themselves: the changing demands placed upon them is leading them to seek a school-based culture of professional development. Moving from INSET towards professional development has meant recognising that, while INSET was often voluntary and reflected individual needs, professional development is regarded as essential and is almost compulsory on occasion, and while much teacher-focused work continues there is now a greater emphasis on both teacher and school in combination.

Similar changes are evident in Scotland. In 1985, colleges of education annually provided SED with a retrospective account of their in-service activity, known as INSET XX in the form of a computerised database. This was changed for School Agency Focused In-Service (SAFIS) to a system of prospective approval whereby colleges, in the context of published national priorities, had to negotiate appropriate short courses and programmes with local authority officials and advisers. These were then submitted to SED for approval before being offered. At the same time, an effort was made to increase productivity in the area of school-focused or agency in-service. Traditionally, there had been a one-for-one arrangement between preparation and contact for college lecturers. The SED argued that much of this activity was repeatable – indeed that was one of the criteria applied to prospective approval – and therefore a reduced amount of preparation time was tenable. A formulaic approach was imposed and lecturer FTE was calculated by taking the number of contact hours and assuming an additional one-third of preparation time plus travel time, based on the notion that lecturers travelled constantly at the sedate pace of 33 mph! The emphasis was on school-related or school-based provision and colleges by this device were to relate more closely to the perceived needs and plans of local authorities.

By session 1989-90, even such prospective planning and agreement of provision was regarded as lacking true consumer-centred qualities and it was announced that the system would move to a 'cash-driven model'. The Department decided to enlarge its specific grant approach to include the bulk of the monies still provided for staffing to colleges of education. Money was to be bid for directly by local authorities, who would provide 25% of the costs and be reimbursed the remaining 75% by the Department. In turn, local authorities would use such grant money to pay colleges and other providers for their services. To facilitate an orderly progression to a full 'market economy' and to allow colleges to transfer to this model, a three-year period of 'ring-fencing' for the colleges was established. This meant that initially local authorities had to spend at least 90% of this specific grant with the colleges and this was progressively reduced to zero by 1993-94. Difficulties were experienced in certain areas of the country as a result of non-payment of community charge and local authorities in some instances found it difficult to fund the initial 25% of costs that would permit them to access grant. This, in turn, created financial difficulties for colleges. Moray House has managed to weather this period of change to funding by continuing to provide quality consultancy and staff development to meet both local and national needs. The Institute has engaged with and listened closely to those planning staff development and acted accordingly (McMichael and Boyle, 1994).

Moray House Involvement in Consultancy Activities

Throughout the period teachers have had clear expectations that support for curriculum and other changes will be provided at both national and local levels. Such 'multiple innovation' (Stronach and Morris, 1994) has been nourished by a variety of local in-service and staff development support allied with the national production of curriculum materials and staff development or training opportunities (O'Brien and McGettrick, 1995; McMichael and Boyle, 1994). As a result, continuing professional development in Scottish schools is now rarely an isolated process: the trend is for teachers to work occasionally in school clusters or together in departmental or cross-disciplinary teams. Such efforts will be invariably noted in the portable individual record of staff development recommended by the National Guidelines for Staff Development and Appraisal.

The range of developments since the introduction of curriculum reforms following the Munn and Dunning Reports has been characterised by the tendency to follow a central – local pattern of determining guidelines and providing associated staff development and support. Such changes have required in-school accommodation if not promotion of the innovation and has necessitated from a head teacher's perspective 'three strands of development' that are interdependent: curriculum development, staff development and institutional development (Harrison and Macintosh, 1989).

Moray House Institute staff have been involved in supporting each of these strands because of the continuing provision of professional consultancy and in-service or staff development provided by lecturers at national and local level. This provision continues to be funded by SOED although, as noted above, the funding model has altered dramatically in the past few years. Over the years provision has become increasingly planned to meet not only the needs of teachers and schools, but also the national system needs through the deployment of staff as consultants on national tasks (Kirk, 1988). Such support has related closely to national policy initiatives because the practice of determining national priorities and focusing resources on specific developments has become increasingly sophisticated in recent years.

Many Moray House staff have contributed to such national consultancy and local initiatives in the past decade, and not only in teacher education. A range of short course approaches focusing on the identified professional needs of social workers, and now funded in a similar way to teacher education consultancy, has been recently developed by Ian Mallinson and his colleagues in Social Work. Lyn Tett, Director of Community Education, and her colleagues are increasingly in demand at local and national level to provide consultancy and management for the national programme on performance indicators, for example. It is in teacher education, however, that the bulk of consultancy has been concentrated.

There have been few initiatives in the last 10 years which have not involved Moray House staff in a significant way at national level. A range of staff contributed to Standard Grade support as National Development Officers, while today similar expertise from the Institute has been recognised for the Higher Still reforms by the appointment of Ian Bonner-Evans in Religious and Moral Education, Pauline Sangster in English, Douglas Buchanan in Chemistry, and Alison Closs in Special Educational Needs as NDOs. Jim Wight of the Management Development Unit and other colleagues such as Sylvia Jackson and Hugh Perfect were fully involved in the development and subsequent delivery of the SOED modules and related resources for head teacher training, while Janet Draper, Frank Adams and Jim O'Brien have made substantial contributions in the design and delivery of the national training provision for Staff Development and Appraisal. At local level and with other professions similar themes were taken up by Dave Turner and Jim Kidd, who also involved himself with appraisal training for lighthouse keepers! The Institute, through Tony van der Kuyl and his associates at the Scottish Interactive Technology Centre (SITC), developed the Interactive Video disk 'Skills for Appraisal Interviewing', which has been very well received in schools (TESS, 1994), and which has won a number of international awards. SITC has also been successful in attracting consultancy funds from the European Union in the last few years.

There has been a range of consultancy offered in the expressive arts, building on the earlier work done by Charlie MacQueen and Archie McIntosh in 1986, with consultancy being completed at the moment by Amanda Gizzi and Tony Gemmell in relation to a CD-ROM resource for visual art. Physical education has contributed to the Institute's consultancy record, particularly in relation to collaborative work with the Consultative Committee on the Curriculum and the Scottish Examination Board. Standard Grade and Higher Grade Physical Education have benefited as a result, while the 5-14 Programme has been supported too through Eileen Carnegie's contribution to CDi resources. In other curricular areas involvement has been no less with, for example, the major initiative to establish Modern Languages in Primary Schools which has involved Richard Easton in substantial national and local consultancy. Computing and Information Technology colleagues have continued the parallel approach of producing quality resources and, in the Social Subjects, the RESST (Resources for Environmental Studies Teaching) approach begun a decade ago still prospers. It is impossible to refer to all the consultancy offered by staff and those mentioned are only illustrative of the wide-ranging efforts of Moray House staff whose commitment to supporting professional development has not been diminished by the structural and funding changes described.

The difference between consultancy and research is often difficult to detect and Paquita McMichael has been very active in general areas of staff development and in the particular field of gifted children. Special Educational Needs staff have provided a range of consultancies to schools and at national level, while maintaining an impressive portfolio of courses and modules which is second to none in Scotland. Particular specialisms held by staff such as Marianna Buultjens and Helen Mitchell from the Scottish Sensory Centre are in demand, and other centres which have emerged in the last decade such as CERES in the field of multi-cultural and anti-racist education and equal opportunities or the Centre for Dyslexia offer a range of services which are valued throughout the country.

A Way Ahead?

Today, the market place dominates in-service and staff development provision. Increasingly, as local authorities anticipate the possible effects of legislation to move to single-tier authorities in 1996, their own traditional advisory services are under review with the potential that they, too, will be obliged to compete for the available funding. Since

1989, the Institute has worked even more closely with local authorities throughout Scotland, but particularly with Fife, the Borders and Lothian, to plan and provide appropriate opportunities for teacher and school development. Local authorities have been prime agents in identifying needs and determining appropriate providers to meet such needs. To date, Moray House has been an instrumental provider. The moves to devolved school management mean that increasing sums of money are to be allocated to individual schools for staff development purposes. This perhaps suggests a possible change in strategy and focus for the Institute in accessing funds through participant fees rather than consultancy contracts with education authorities. The Professional Development Centre (PDC), established in 1993-94 to support the marketing and administration of the Institute's consultancy and the developing Modular Master's Scheme, as well as Institute staff, will be devoting considerable time in the future to the enhancement of our relationships with individual schools and teachers. While continuing to work and plan with education authority colleagues and advisers, we will be seeking greater co-operation with individual or clusters of schools in the identification of needs which might then be addressed in ways which are effective and economical for teachers and schools. Hargreaves' vision of the 'learning school' or agency, which he regards as the logical conclusion of the range of changes of the last decade, offers Moray House a continuing opportunity to support through consultancy the continuing development needs of the professions we serve. That consultancy will require to be planned in a relationship of professional partnership with our clients, and provided the quality of our work is evident, the Institute may continue to prosper and offer the service necessary to enhance the effectiveness of the professions in times of continuing change.

References

Alexander, E., Havard, J. *et al.* (1992). *Developing School Managers: Interchange No. 4*, Research and Intelligence Unit SOED.

Brown, S. (1992). 'Raising Standards: factors influencing the effectiveness of innovations.' *Critical Reflections on Curriculum Policy: The SCRE Fellowship Lectures* 1992: 7-27.

Brown, S. (1994). 'School effectiveness research and the evaluation of schools.' *Evaluation and Research in Education* 8, Nos. 1 and 2: 55-68.

Brown, S. and Munn, P. (Eds.) (1985). *The Changing Face of Education 14-16: Curriculum and Assessment*. NFER-Nelson.

Gilbert, C., Ed. (1990). *Local Management of Schools: A Guide for Governors and Teachers*. Books for Teachers. Kogan Page.

Goulder, J., Simpson, M., *et al.* (1994). 'The 5-14 Development Programme in Scottish secondary schools: the first phase.' *The Curriculum Journal* Vol. 5 (No. 1): 69-81.

Hargreaves, D. and Hopkins, D. (1991). *The Empowered School: The Management and Practice of Development Planning.* Cassell.

Hargreaves, D. H. (1994). 'The New Professionalism: The synthesis of professional and institutional development.' *Teaching and Teacher Education* Vol. 10 (No. 4): 423-438.

Harlen, W. and Malcolm, H. (1994). 'Putting the curriculum and assessment guidelines in place in Scottish primary schools.' *The Curriculum Journal* Vol. 5 (No. 1): 55-67.

Harrison, C. and Macintosh M. (1989). *Managing Change: The Headteacher's Perspective.* Scottish Academic Press.

Hartley, D. (1994). 'Devolved school management: the "new deal" in Scottish education.' *Journal of Education Policy* 9 (No. 2): 129-140.

Kirk, G. (1988). *Teacher Education and Professional Development.* Scottish Academic Press.

Kirk, G. and Cameron-Jones, M. (1994). The Education of Teachers in Scotland: Changes and Challenges. *Current Changes and Challenges in European Teacher Education* (Ed.) T. Sander, Bruxelles, RIF: Reseau d'Institutions de Formation - Sub Network 4.

Macbeth, A. M. (1990). *School Boards: From Purpose to Practice.* Scottish Academic Press.

McMichael, P. and Boyle, S. (1994). *A review of development in the Nursery, Primary and Special Education Sectors,* Lothian Regional Council, Department of Education.

Newton, C. and Tarrant, T. (1992). *Managing Change in Schools.* Routledge.

O'Brien, J. and McGettrick, B. J. (1995 forthcoming). *Support for Curriculum Development: What do secondary teachers value in times of great curricular change?,* St Andrew's College.

Perfect, H. (1985). Professional development of teachers. *Moray House and Professional Education, 1835-1985* G. Kirk, (Ed.). Scottish Academic Press. 69-78.

Ransom, S. (1990). *The Politics of Reorganizing Schools.* Unwin Hyman.

Roger, A. and Hartley, D., (Eds.) (1990). *Curriculum and Assessment in Scotland: A Policy for the 90's.* Scottish Academic Press.

SED (1989). *Learning and Teaching in TVEI in Scotland: A Report by HM Inspectors of Schools,* HMSO, Scottish Education Department.

SOED (1992). *Devolved School Management: Guidelines for Progress,* The Scottish Office Education Department.

SOED (1994). *Higher Still: Opportunity for All,* The Scottish Office.

Stronach, I. and Morris, B. (1994). 'Polemical Notes on Educational Evaluation in the Age of "Policy Hysteria".' *Evaluation and Research in Education* 8 (Nos. 1 and 2): 5-19.

TESS (1994). Thumbs down for in-service resources. *TESS.* September 16, 1994.

List of Contributors

All contributors are on the staff of Moray House
Institute of Education

David M. Bayman is Director of the Scottish Centre for Physical Education, Movement and Leisure Studies.

Professor Margot Cameron-Jones is Director of Teacher Education.

Brian D. Cosford is Senior Lecturer in Staff Development.

Fernando Almeida Diniz is Head of the Department of Professional Development and Community Education.

Professor Gordon Kirk is Principal.

John Landon is Senior Lecturer and Co-ordinator of the Modular Master's Scheme.

Ian Mallinson is Director of Social Work Education.

Robert W. McNie is Senior Lecturer in Open Learning.

James W. Morrison is Director of the Scottish Centre for International Education.

James O'Brien is Vice-Principal.

Hugh E. Perfect is Senior Assistant Principal.

Donald Skinner is Senior Lecturer in Theory and Practice of Teaching.

Lyn Tett is Director of Community Education.